Giant Book of Optical Puzzles

By Keith Kay, Charles H. Paraquin,
Michael A. DiSpezio, Katherine Joyce,
E. Richard Churchill, and Larry Evans

Main Street
A division of Sterling Publishing Co., Inc.
New York

Material in this collection was adapted from

Little Giant Book of Optical Illusions
© Keith Kay
World's Best Optical Illusions
© Charles H. Paraquin
Visual Thinking Puzzles
© Michael A. DiSpezio
How to Make Optical Illusions
© E. Richard Churchill
Astounding Optical Illusions
© Katherine Joyce
Lateral Logic Mazes for the Serious Player
© Larry Evans
3-Dimensional Lateral Logic Mazes
© Larry Evans
Little Giant Book of Optical Tricks
© Keith Kay

10 9 8 7 6 5 4 3 2

© 2003 by Sterling Publishing Co., Inc.
Published by Sterling Publishing Co., Inc.
387 Park Avenue South, New York, NY 10016
Distributed in Canada by Sterling Publishing
C/o Canadian Manda Group, One Atlantic Avenue, Suite 105
Toronto, Ontario, Canada M6K 3E7
Distributed in Great Britain by Chrysalis Books
64 Brewery Road, London N7 9NT, England
Distributed in Australia by Capricorn Link (Australia) Pty. Ltd.
P.O. Box 704, Windsor, NSW 2756, Australia

Manufactured in the United States of America

Sterling ISBN 1-4027-1051-8

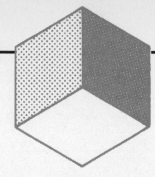

Table of Contents

Optical
Illusions

Optical illusions are pictures that play tricks on your eyes and baffle your perception. They are not the result of faulty vision or psychic suggestion. Depending on light, viewing angle, or the way the picture is drawn, we may see things that aren't there—and often don't see what's right under our nose. Why does it happen?

Sometimes the answer lies in the way our eyes work. When we use both eyes, we see an object from two slightly set-apart angles. Each one registers a different view. If we use only one eye, look what happens:

Close your left eye. Keep your right eye focused on the dog and move the book back and forth in front of you. At one point, the cat disappears completely. You have just found your blind spot. Everyone has one. It is the spot where the optic nerve cord leaves your eye, and there are no nerve cells to register an image. If you use both eyes as you look at the dog, you won't have a blind spot. The image from your left eye will make up for the blank in your right.

The shortcomings of our vision explain some types of optical illusions, but not all of them. Our eyes gather impressions, but it is the brain that interprets them. And the brain is always trying to make sense out of what it sees. So in spite of the fact that we know how perspective works, we go to the theatre or the movies and imagine that we're in a different world, tricked by a stage set and special effects. We watch magic acts and believe what reflecting mirrors show us. Illusion is everywhere—in art and architecture, in fashion and advertising, in the street and on television, even in the supermarket. If our eyes see something that the brain can't figure out, our minds "correct" the picture automatically.

Here is another illusion:

The box in the first picture contains an ordinary circle. The second box contains a field of slanted lines. Put them together and look what happens. The circle appears to become an oval and the box seems to be completely lop-sided. Test them with a ruler and compass. You'll see that they are exactly the same as they were before.

The human eye isn't as perfect as a camera lens, but that doesn't mean it is defective—just the opposite. Its adaptability is its strongpoint. In the semi-dark, for instance, our eyes function amazingly well. After about half an hour, our vision completely adjusts to the dark and its sensitivity increases 50,000 times! In the dark, we can see a burning candle from nearly 20 miles (32 kilometers) away!

Birds of prey (eagles and hawks) have much better vision than humans do in daylight. They see farther, but they suffer from night-blindness. Some other animals (owls, hedgehogs, cats) see well at night, but do not have very keen eyesight. So as human beings, we are lucky. We can see reasonably well during both day and night.

Humans are not the only ones who are tricked by optical illusions, either. Laboratory tests performed on fish and birds lead to the startling conclusion that these animals are fooled just about as often as we are, and sometimes in the same way!

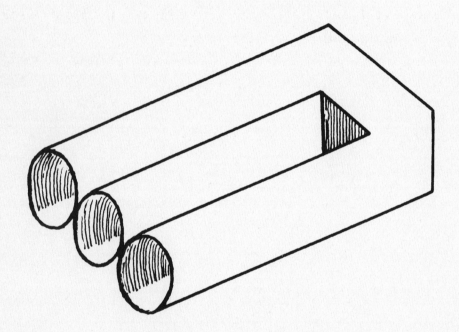

Deception? Illusion? Or just a careless artist?

Scientists have studied optical illusions for centuries, but they still don't agree about how or why all of them work. You'll see many different types of illusions in this book—geometric tricks, physiological tricks and psychological illusions—and you'll learn how many of them operate. But by no means are these *all* the optical illusions that are possible. The number of tricks you can play on your eyes is almost inexhaustible. These illusions are simply meant to amuse you, inspire you to explore this delightful scientific hobby yourself, and perhaps even invent some new illusions of your own.

One suggestion: as you turn to each picture, look at it first with your naked eye. Don't check it out with a ruler or tracing paper until afterwards—when you can't believe your eyes!

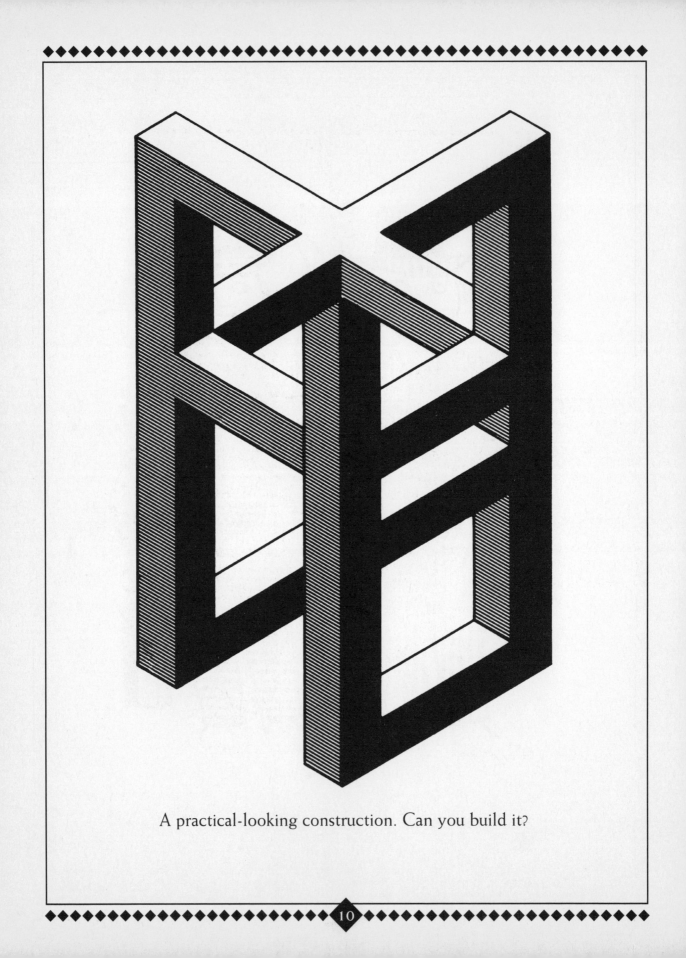

A practical-looking construction. Can you build it?

Twin brothers: one of them has a bigger appetite. Which one?

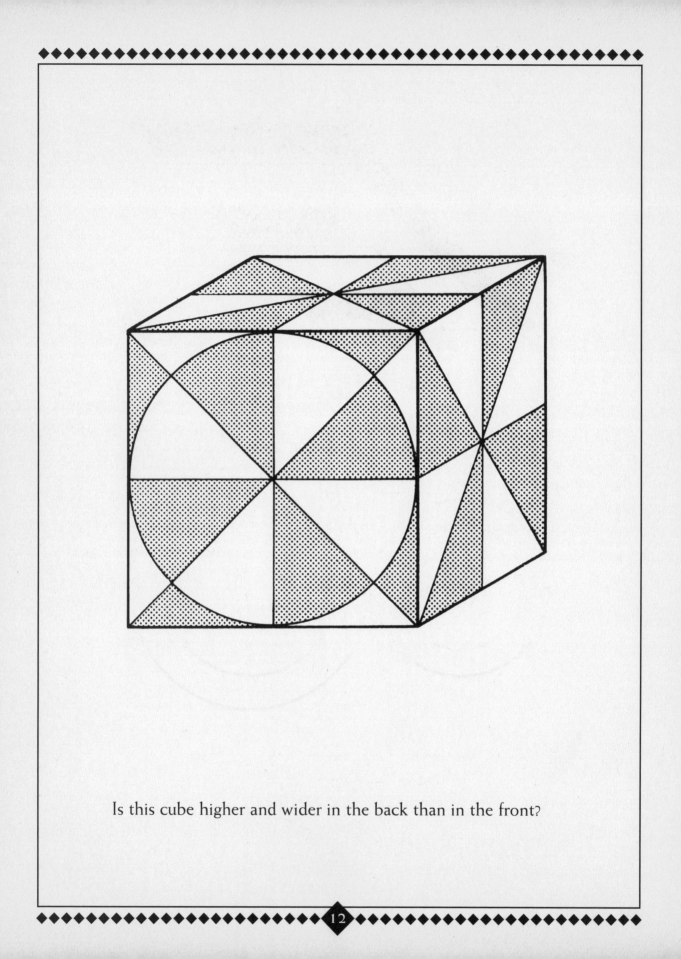

Is this cube higher and wider in the back than in the front?

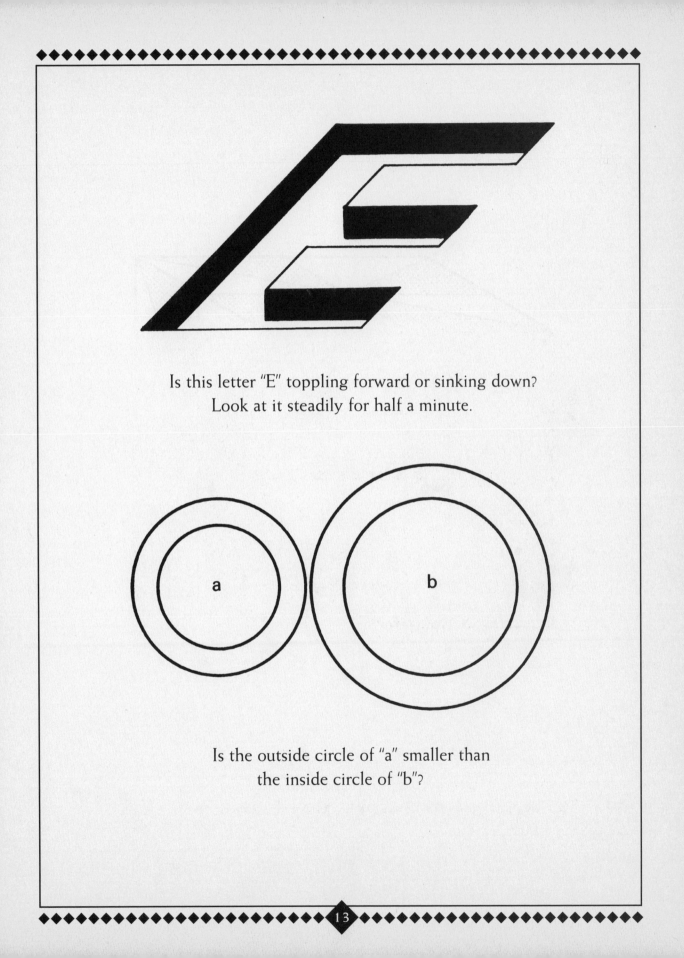

Is this letter "E" toppling forward or sinking down?
Look at it steadily for half a minute.

Is the outside circle of "a" smaller than
the inside circle of "b"?

Which of these movie-goers is the tallest?

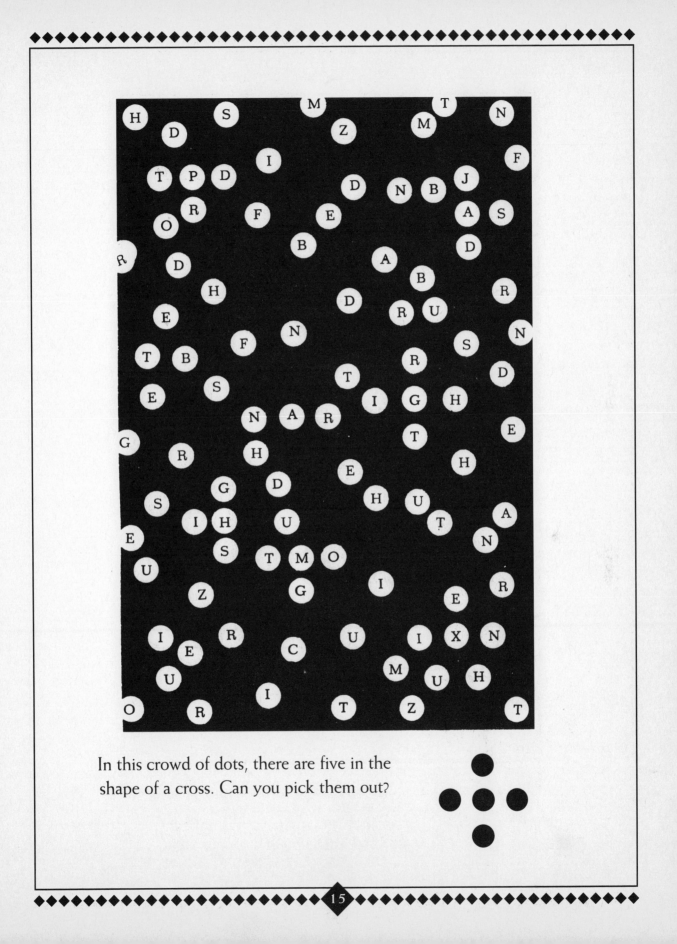

In this crowd of dots, there are five in the shape of a cross. Can you pick them out?

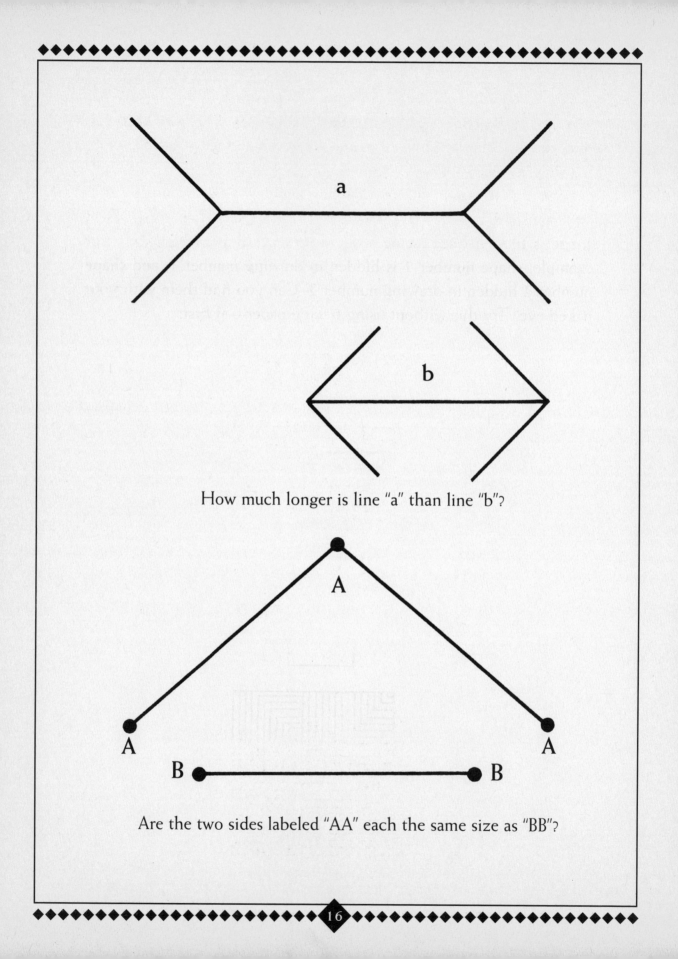

How much longer is line "a" than line "b"?

Are the two sides labeled "AA" each the same size as "BB"?

Look at the shapes at the bottom of this page. If anyone told you that you wouldn't be able to find them—even though you were looking right at them—would you believe it?

The drawings that follow show how difficult it can be to see familiar shapes and figures when they are in unfamiliar surroundings. Each shape is hidden once (same size) in its corresponding diagram. For example, shape number 1 is hidden in drawing number 1, and shape number 2 hidden in drawing number 2. Can you find them with your naked eye? Try this without using tracing paper—at first!

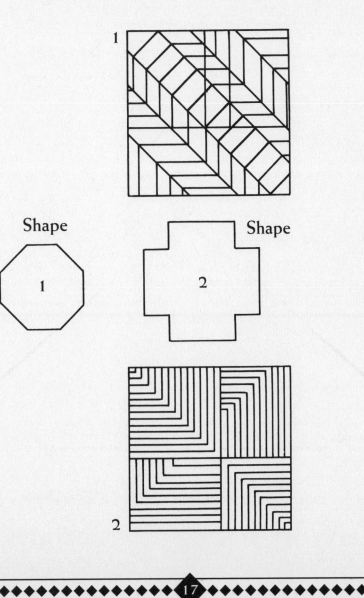

Shape

1

Shape

2

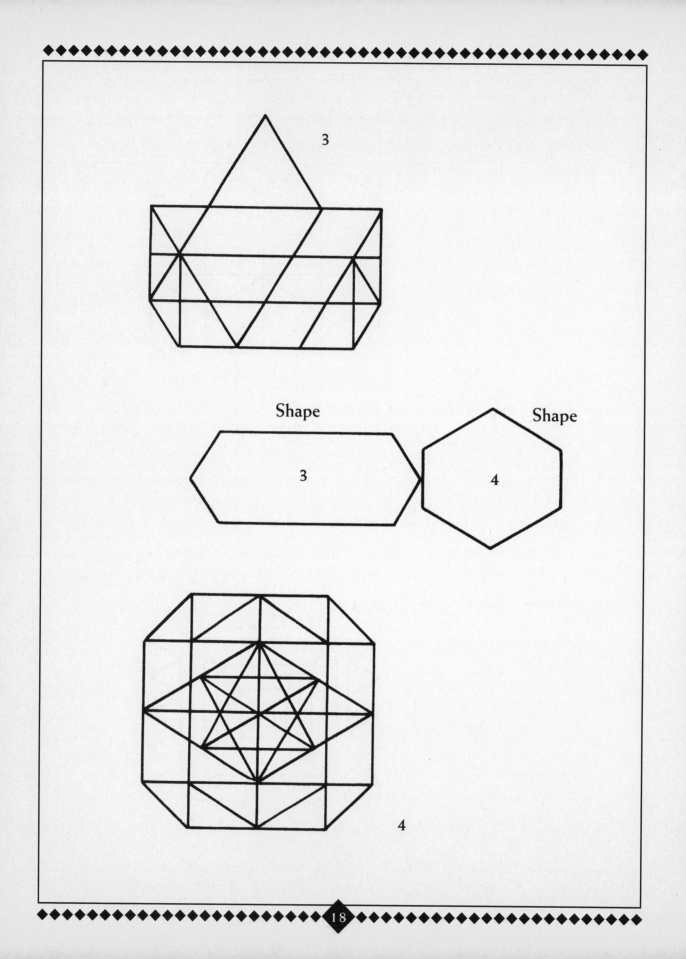

3

Shape

3

Shape

4

4

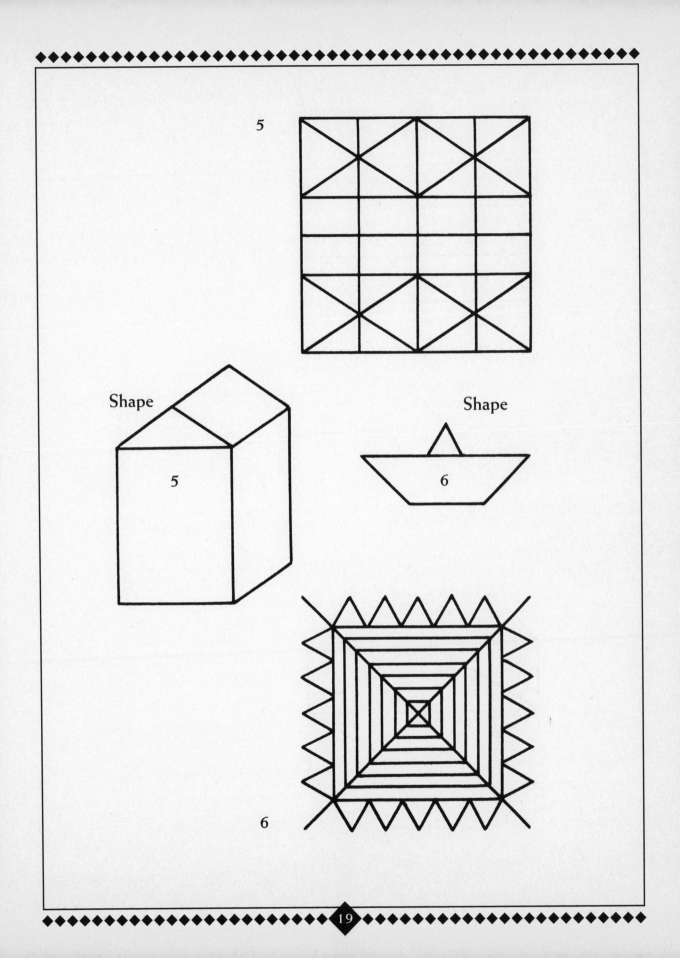

5

Shape

5

Shape

6

6

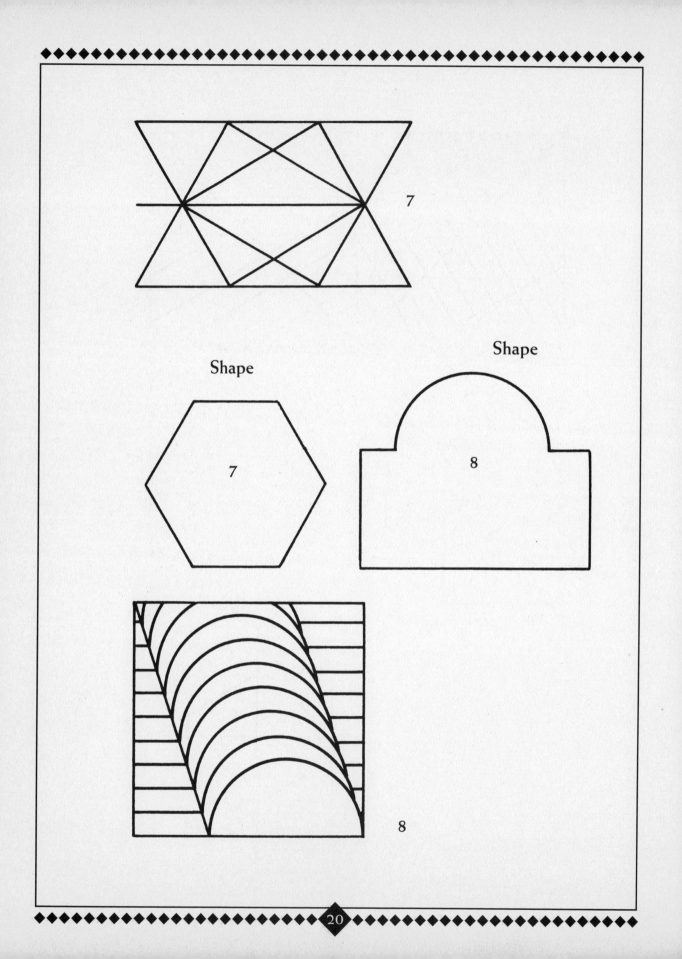

7

Shape

7

Shape

8

8

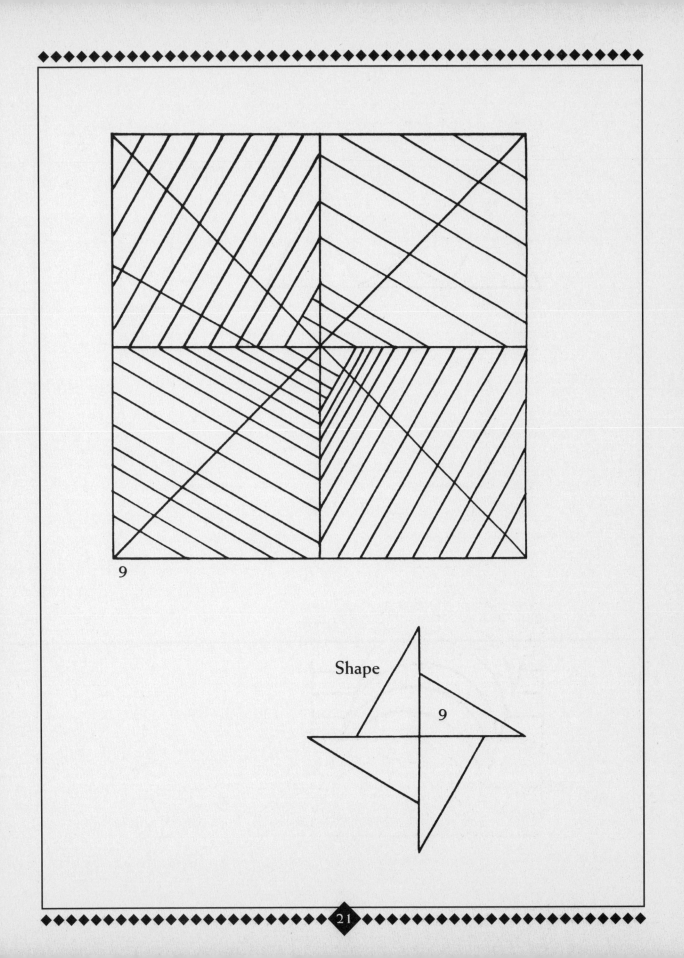

9

Shape

9

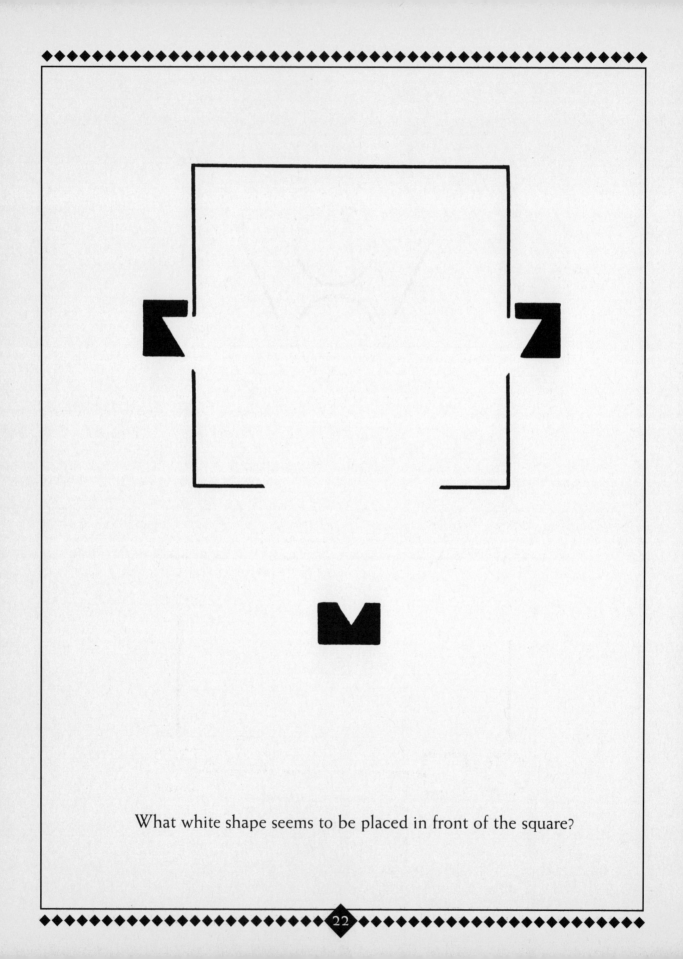

What white shape seems to be placed in front of the square?

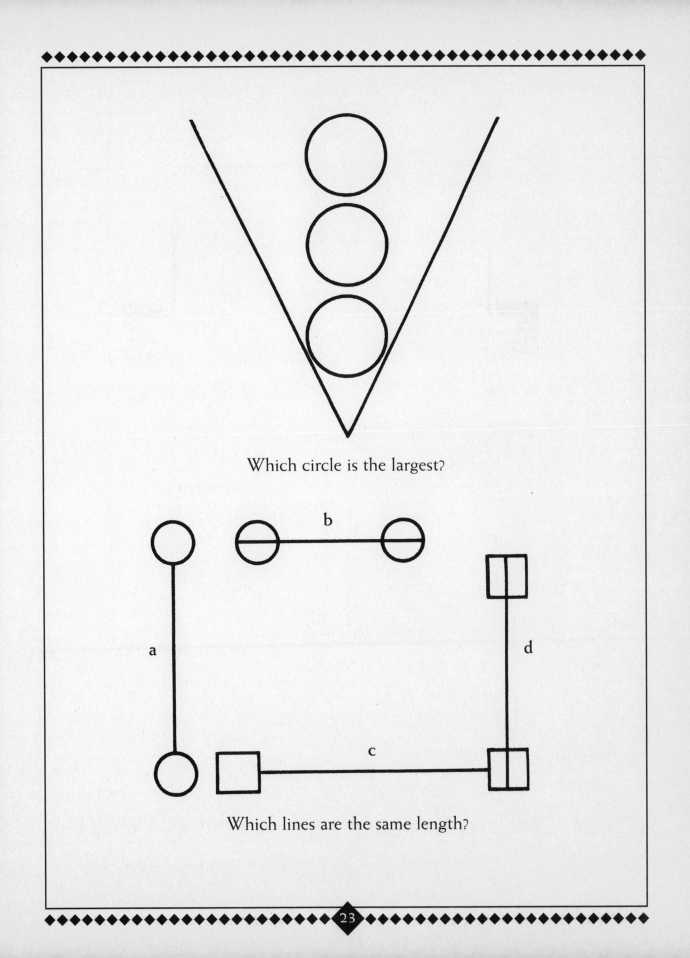

Which circle is the largest?

Which lines are the same length?

a

b

Which of the circles are the same size? Those in row "a"
or those in row "b"?

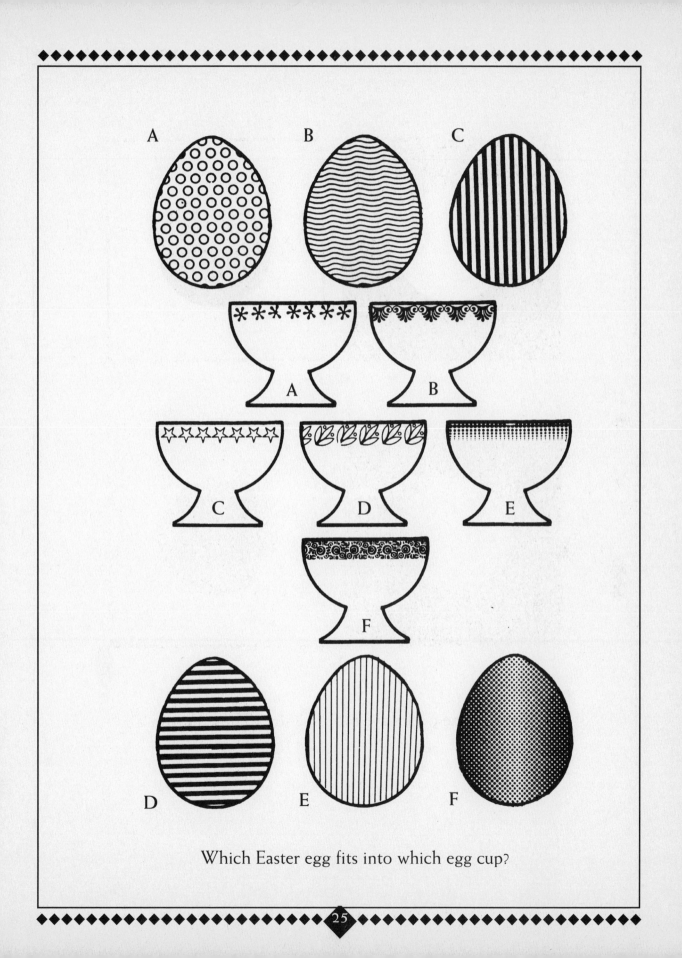

Which Easter egg fits into which egg cup?

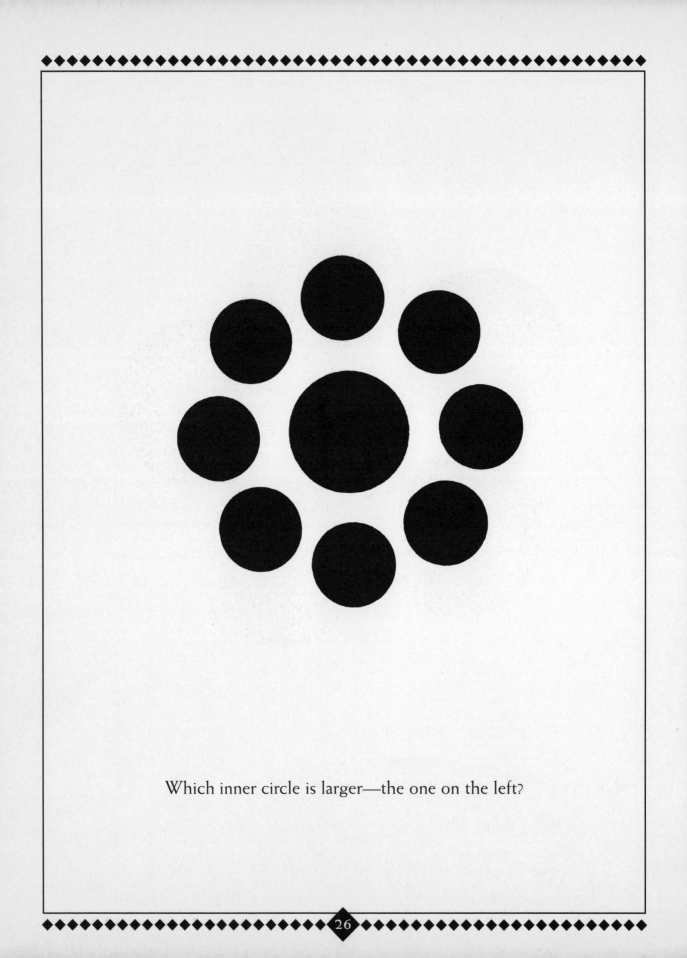

Which inner circle is larger—the one on the left?

Or the one on the right?

Which gray area is brighter?

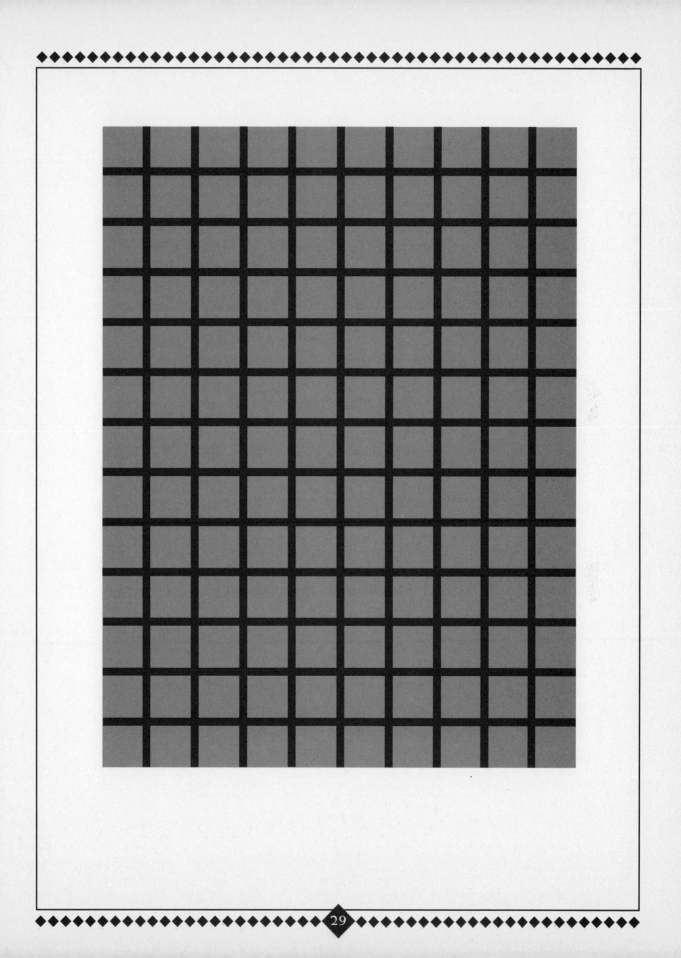

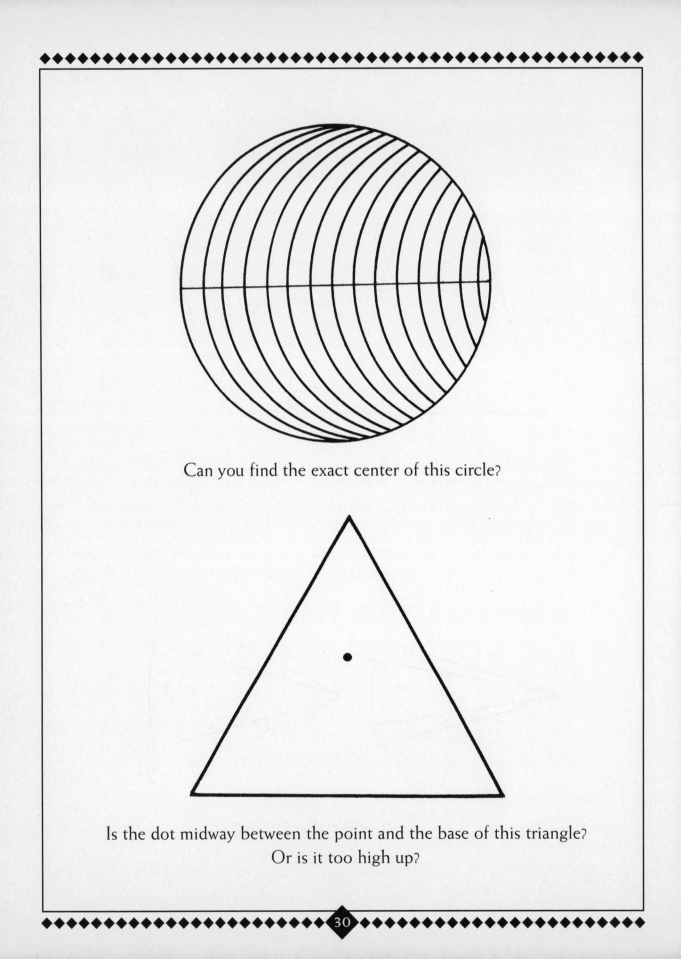

Can you find the exact center of this circle?

Is the dot midway between the point and the base of this triangle?
Or is it too high up?

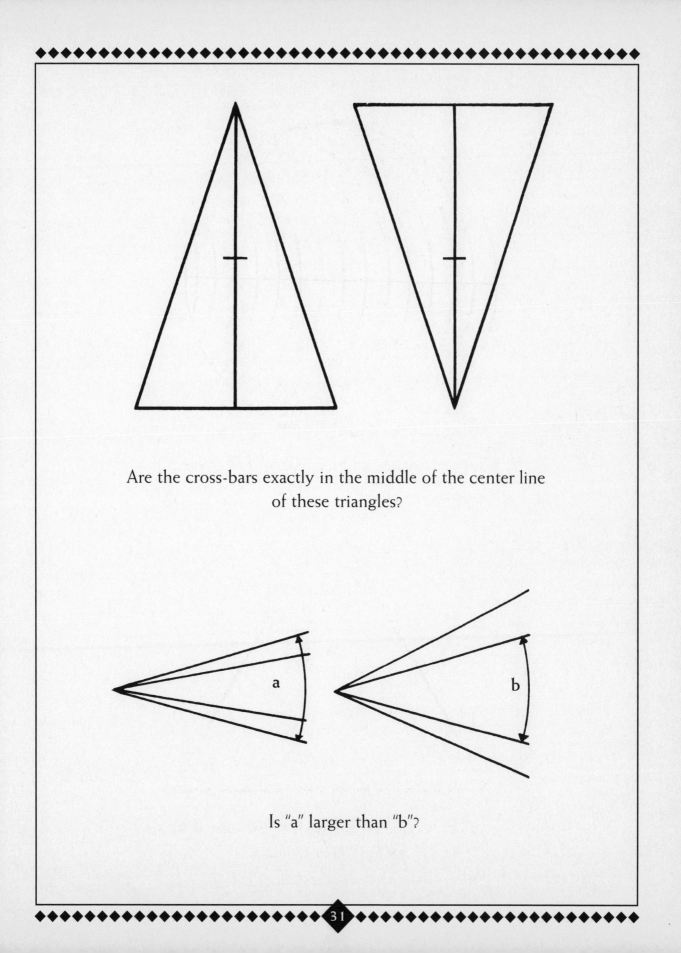

Are the cross-bars exactly in the middle of the center line
of these triangles?

Is "a" larger than "b"?

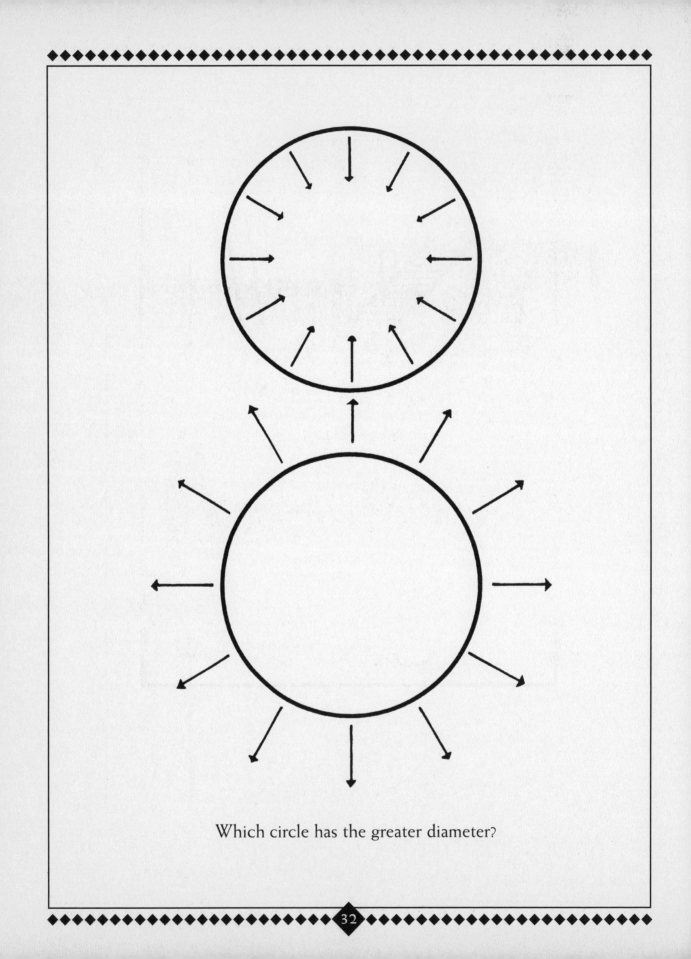

Which circle has the greater diameter?

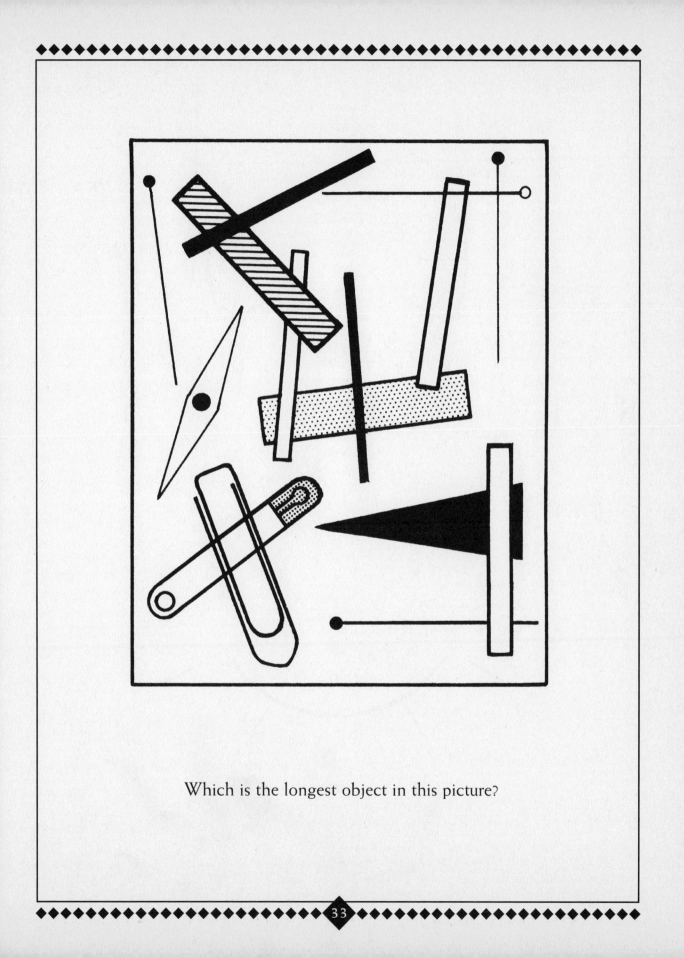

Which is the longest object in this picture?

Visual
Thinking
Puzzles

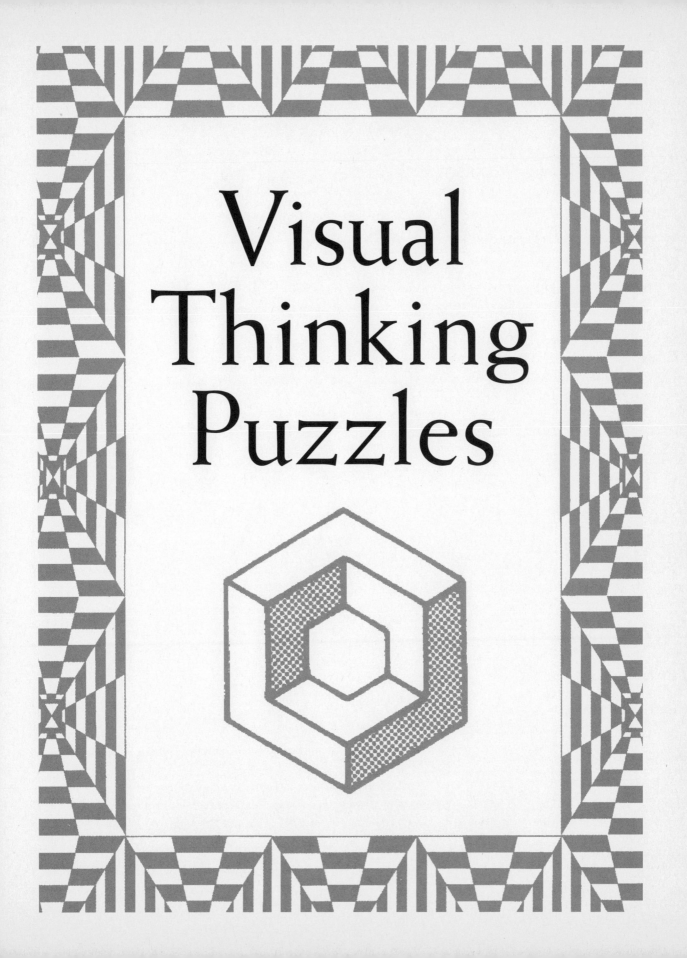

Wrap It Up

You don't need a crystal ball to see into the future. All you need is your brain.

    The shape below is formed from three smaller pieces. These pieces are connected by a tiny hinge at their point of attachment. Suppose you were able to rotate the pieces so the neighboring sides aligned flatly and squarely. Which one of the shapes below could this structure look like?

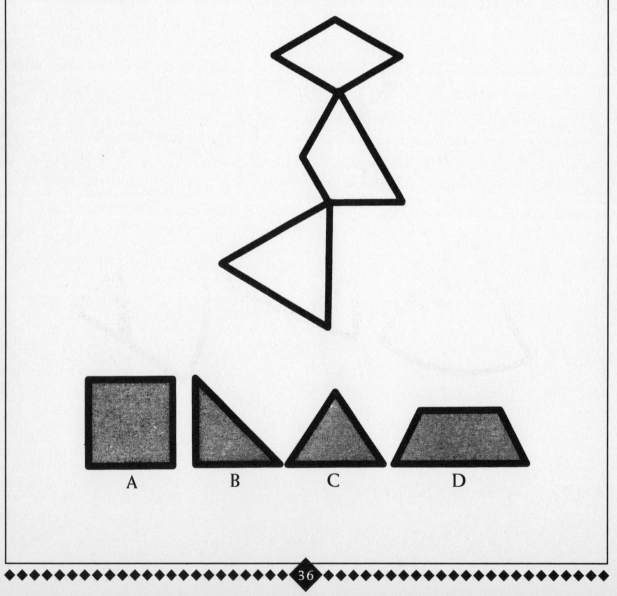

A   B   C   D

Pi Pieces

There are many skills we associate with visual thinking. Some of these skills may be much more difficult to master than others. For example, the ability to mentally rotate objects is often harder than we might imagine.

Try this: If you were to assemble these pieces into a circle, what would the figure formed by the inner lines look like?

Spacing Out

For a moment, let's leave the eye-brain puzzles and just "space out."

A shuttle astronaut leaves her craft to work on a disabled satellite. She lands on one corner of the satellite (which is a perfect cube) and realizes that she must walk across the satellite's surface to the opposite corner. To conserve oxygen, she must follow the shortest possible route. Is her planned route (identified by the dotted line) the shortest path between opposite corners?

Code Caper

What animal is represented in the code below?

Hint: From our earliest years, we learn to identify objects by the space they occupy. Artists, however, sometimes use the space that doesn't occupy something. It's called negative space and it's the fabric that surrounds things. Perhaps a little negative space might help you solve this puzzle?

Cut the Cube

Can you visualize 3-D space? If so, imagine a solid block of clay shaped into a perfect cube. Can you visualize it? Great. Now, let's change it with a modeling knife. How can a single cut produce the six-sided face shown here?

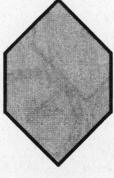

Link Latch

Your optic nerve links the eye and the brain. This "connecting wire" is not passive. As messages travel along its path, visual information is analyzed and sorted. By the time they arrive at the brain, the messages have already been partially processed and analyzed so that no time is wasted.

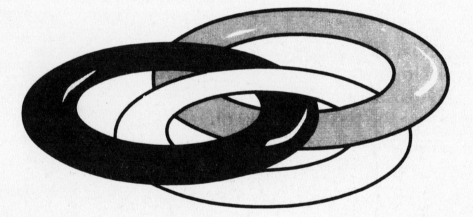

While digging through a box of links, a jeweler uncovers the three joined links shown above. She decides to separate the links. As she examines them, she finds a way to disconnect all three by opening just a single link. Can you?

Amaze in String

A pipe is located at the center of an odd loop of string.

Suppose the string is pulled by its two free ends. Will the string come free of the pipe or will it be caught by it?

Superimposing Position

Suppose the values illustrated by the two graph forms below are added together. Which of the four choices will the combined final graph form look like?

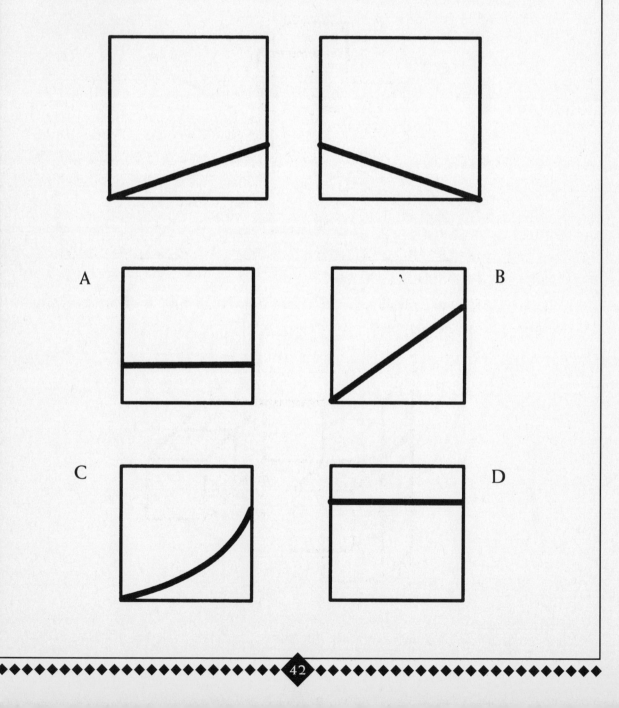

Faces Front

Suppose you can examine this five-block shape (although hidden, the fifth block is present in the middle of the shape) from any angle. How many different cube faces can you count?

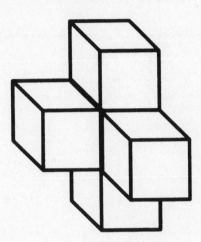

Suppose that hidden block (the fifth one) is evaporated. How many cube faces would now be exposed?

Now examine this nine-block shape from any angle. How many different cube faces can you count?

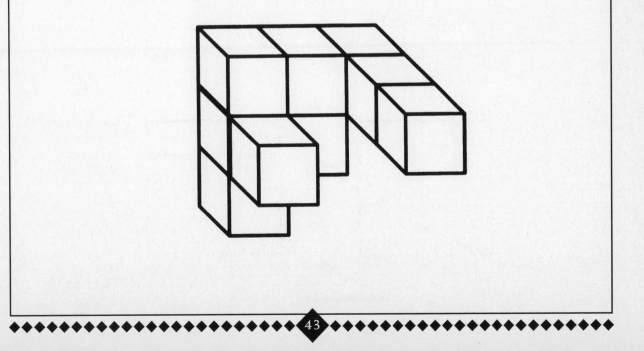

Impossible Profile

Even though you can't see the entire block structure below, you can make accurate statements about its appearance. If viewed from all directions, which one of the four profiles is impossible?

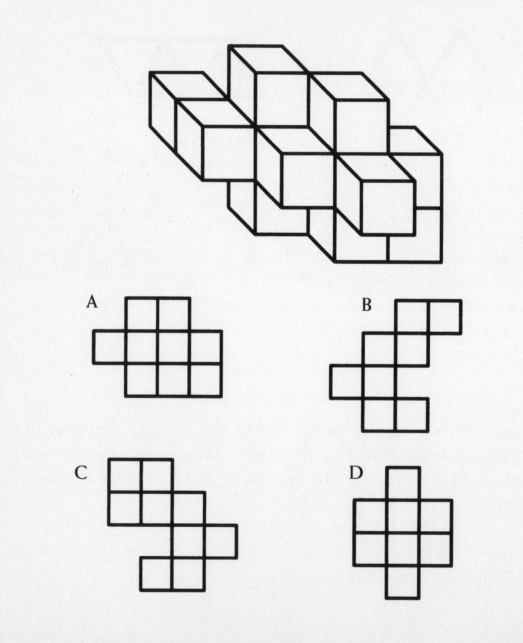

A

B

C

D

Pharaoh Folds

Which of the folding patterns below will produce a shape unlike the others?

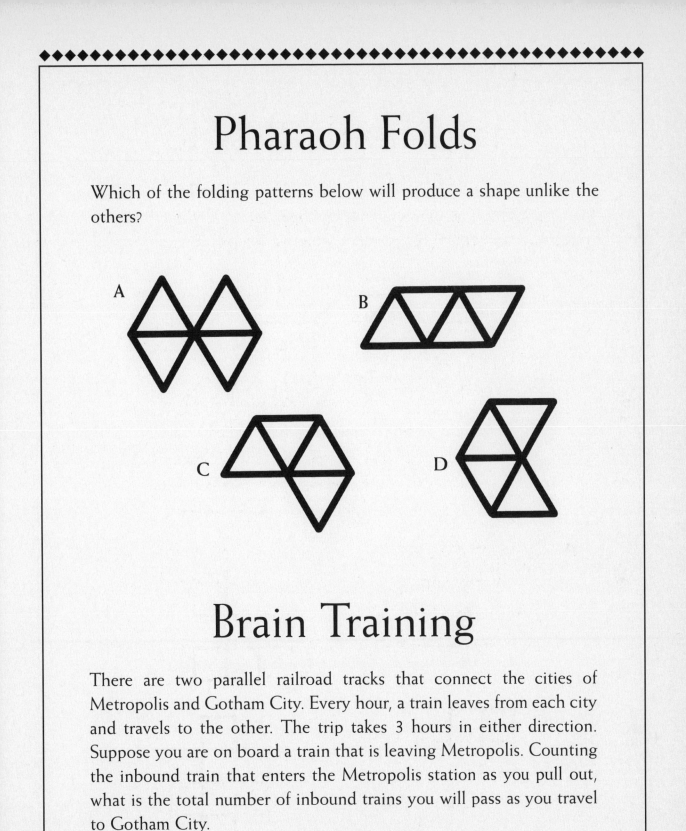

Brain Training

There are two parallel railroad tracks that connect the cities of Metropolis and Gotham City. Every hour, a train leaves from each city and travels to the other. The trip takes 3 hours in either direction. Suppose you are on board a train that is leaving Metropolis. Counting the inbound train that enters the Metropolis station as you pull out, what is the total number of inbound trains you will pass as you travel to Gotham City.

How Many Triangles?

How many equilateral triangles can you uncover
in the pattern below?

On the March

An army of neurotic ants lives in the jungle of some remote country. In their journey they've uncovered a trail formed by three overlapping circles.

Here's the challenge: The ants have to find a route that covers every part of this odd trail. The route can't cross over itself (nor can the ants back up and retrace any steps). Can you uncover their continuous route?

Here's route two with the same restrictions.

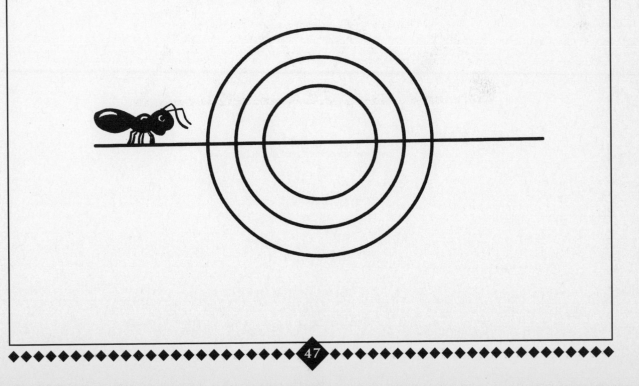

Stop and Think

How many different paths can lead you through the octagonal maze below? From start to finish, you can only move in the direction of the arrows.

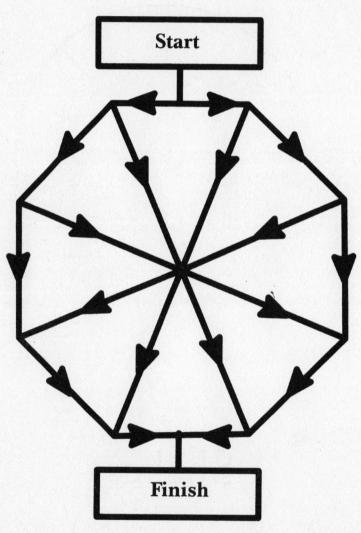

Hint: There is a way to do this puzzle without tracing out each path. Can you uncover the strategy?

Circular Code

What number belongs in the blank slice below?

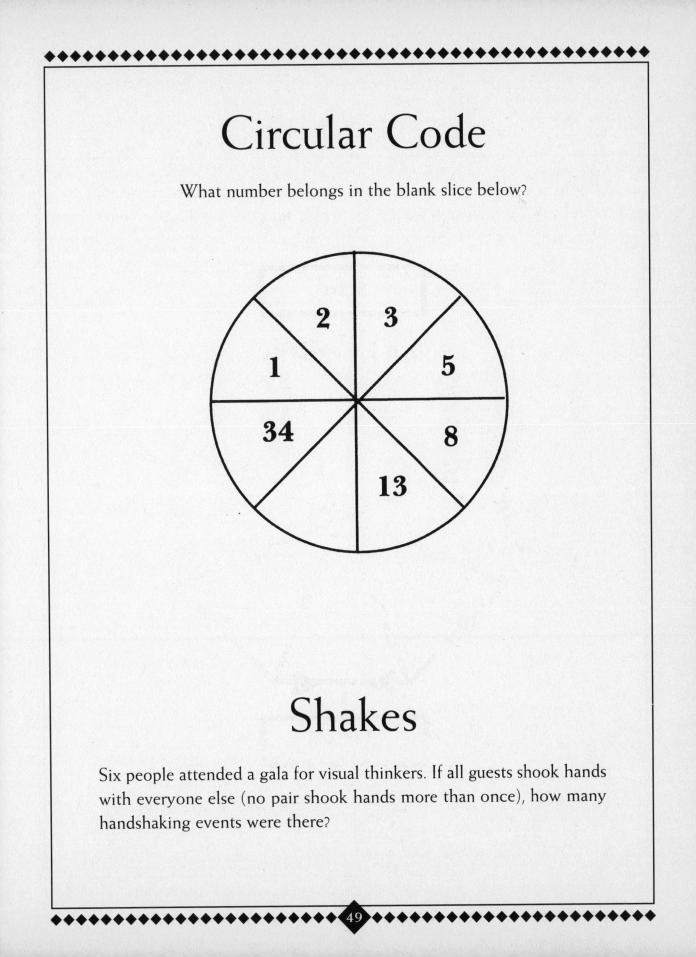

Shakes

Six people attended a gala for visual thinkers. If all guests shook hands with everyone else (no pair shook hands more than once), how many handshaking events were there?

Block Heads

Which pattern of blocks is unlike the others?

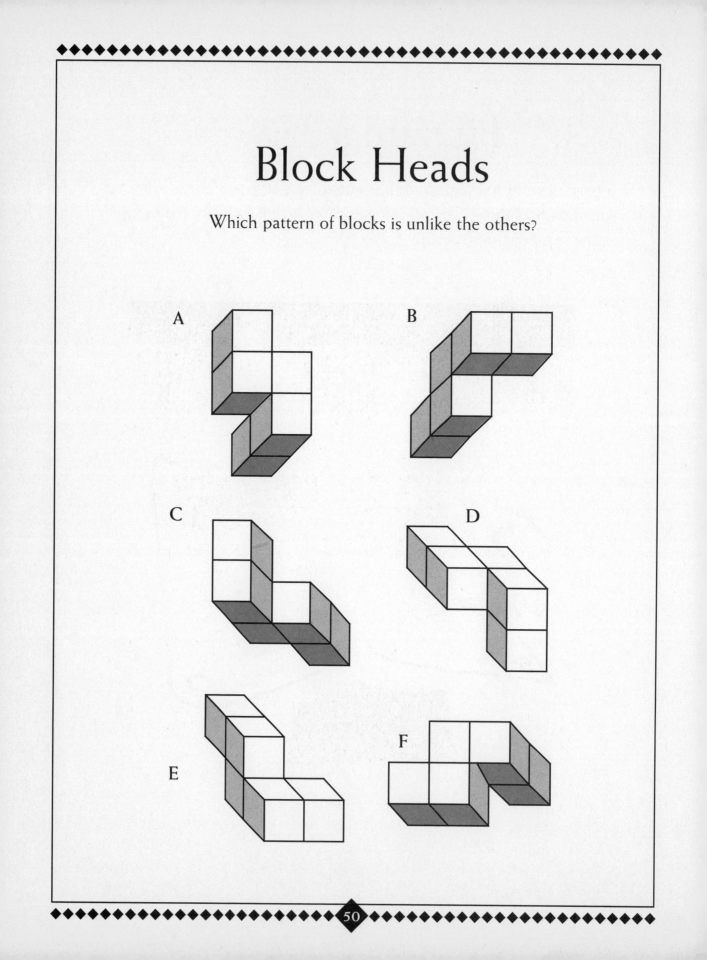

Puzzling Pages

A blast of wind has separated the pages of a local newspaper. From the page numbers shown below, can you determine how many pages were in the complete newspaper?

Controversial Cube

Which two cubes below can be constructed by folding this pattern?
Let's assume that the pattern is the "outside" of the material.

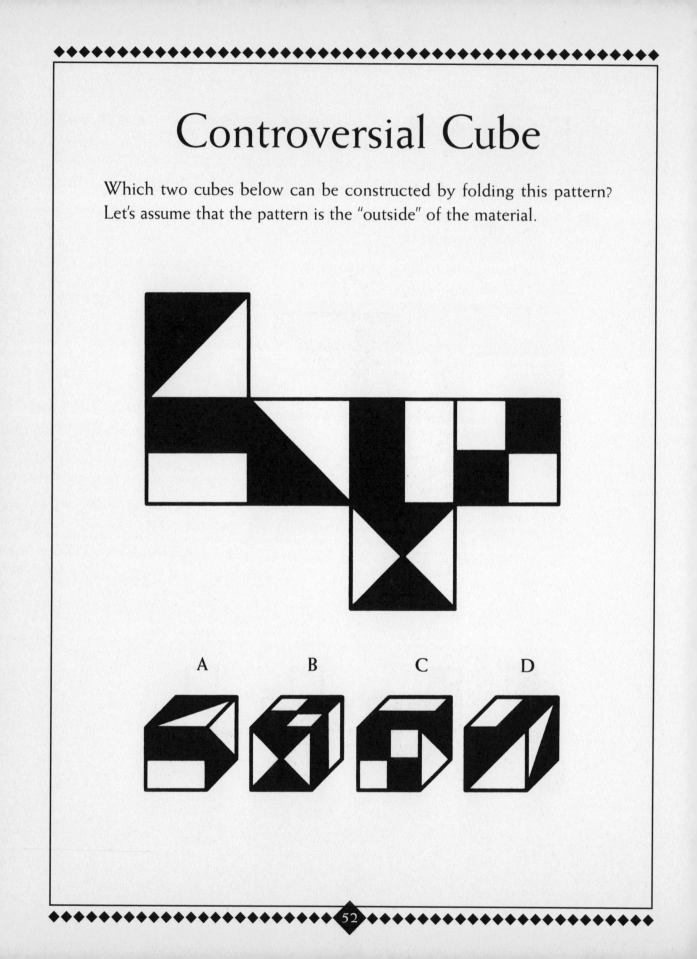

A   B   C   D

From Whence It Came?

Now let's reverse the thinking process. Can you identify the outer pattern from which the cube was folded?

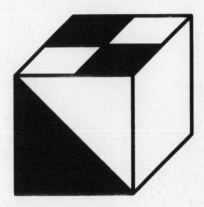

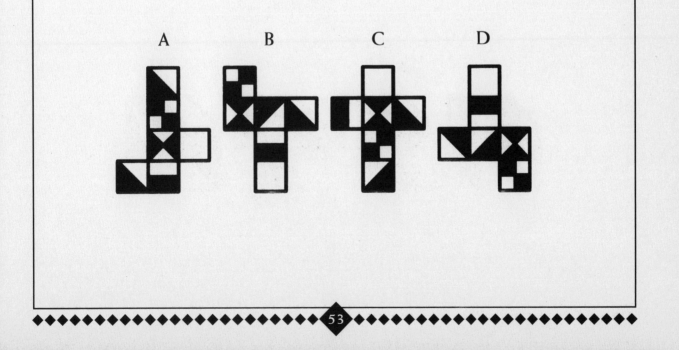

A   B   C   D

Sink Your Teeth

Both cog A and cog D have sixty teeth. Cog B has thirty teeth. Cog C has ten teeth. Suppose cog B makes twenty complete turns every minute. Which will spin faster, cog A or cog D?

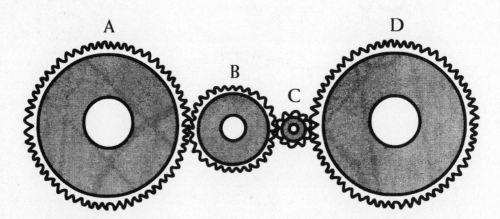

Hands-On/Minds-Off

Examine each of these hands carefully. Then decide which one of the nine is unlike all the others?

Going In Circles?

Are the belts and wheels arranged so that they will spin freely as this mouse races up the treadmill?

Roll With It

If you rolled this pattern into a cylinder, which one of the choices below will it look like?

Dial Dilemma

The instruments in a cockpit are positioned so that a pilot can quickly glance at the indicators and know instantly if there is a problem. In the panel below, one dial does not fit the pattern. Can you locate it quickly?

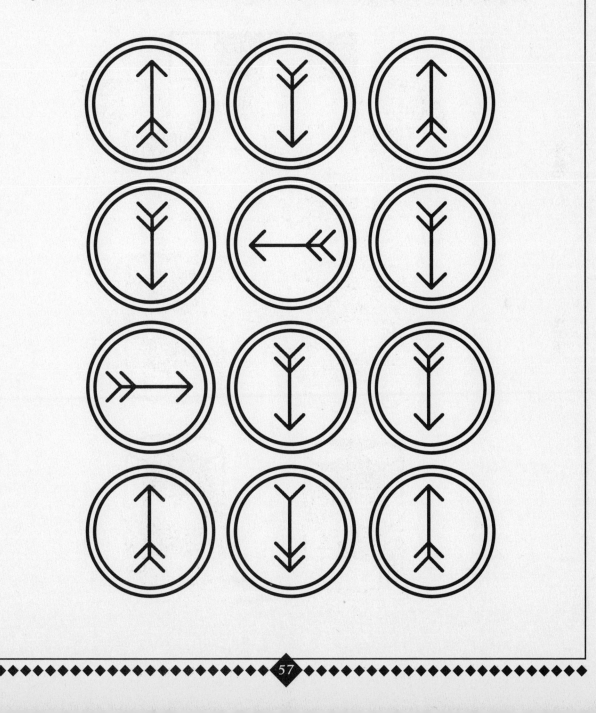

3-D
Mazes

The Barricades

Begin at the IN arrow and remove only TWO barricades to solve the maze.

Almost Straight Down

Enter the maze at any point at the top and follow the black path to the bottom exit. Many paths lead to the exit; however, you may travel upwards only ONCE.

In the Beginning

Begin with the triangle, visit every black circle only once, and then return to the triangle.

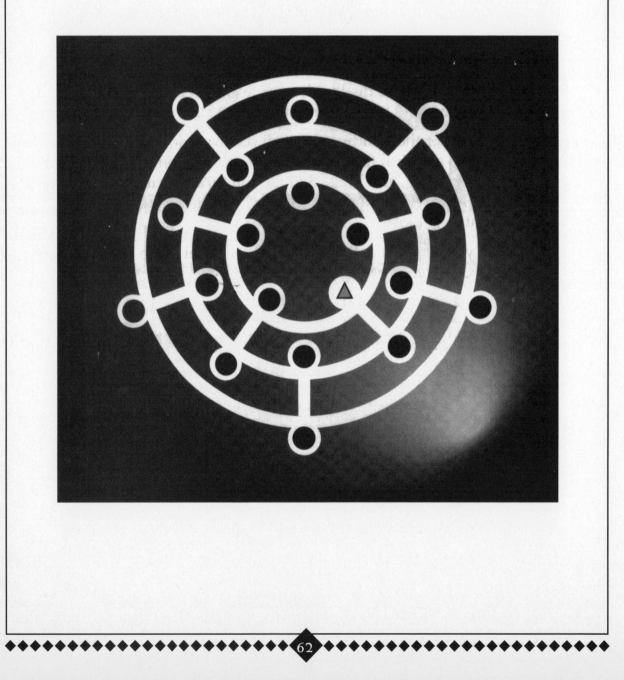

Doors and Stairs

Now that youv'e had a tiny hint of what a Lateral Logic Maze is, let's move on to the next plateau. The next six puzzles ask you to project yourself into the maze and deal with open and closed doors, stairways, upside-down rooms and walls without doors at all.

In the maze on page 64, you enter the building through the front door and proceed into each room in a logical fashion. The maze on page 65 takes you on a bit longer trip through a building, and on page 66 you have three stories of an office building. Be very careful when you climb the stairs on page 66 because you don't want to get lost.

Good luck on your travels in this section. We'll meet again when you reach Solid Geometry.

Walls Only

Begin at the IN arrow and enter each enclosed room only once, then exit. How many doors must you cut?

The House of Mystery

In this mystery-house maze, open only FIVE doors on your way from the IN arrow to the OUT arrow.

The Office Building

Enter the three-story office building at the main entrance and exit at the same place. You must visit all three floors using the stairs. You may only open TWO doors during your visit. Be sure to use the correct stairs!

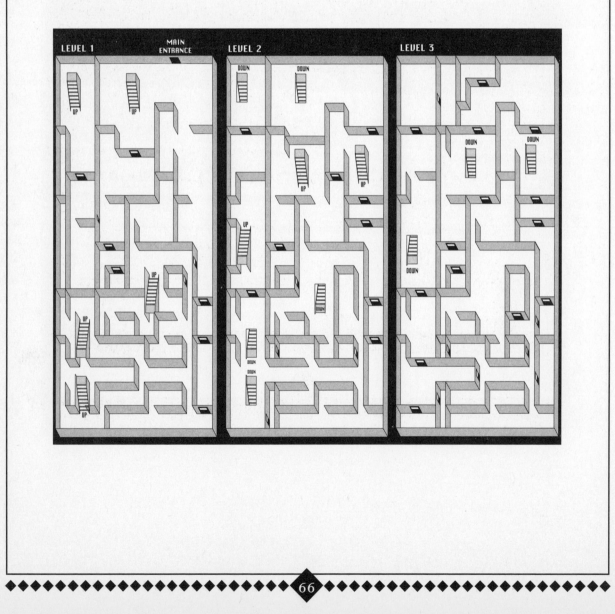

One to Win

Enter the maze and walk through ALL the open doors while opening only ONE closed door. You may pass through each opening only once.

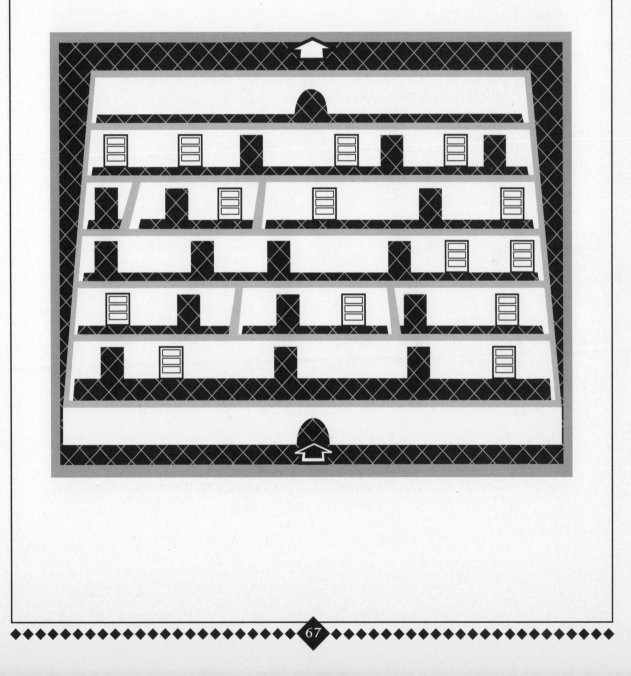

Number Fun

Start with the number 3, in the center of this maze, and travel 3 spaces horizontally or vertically. Then move the number of spaces indicated on the NEW square. Work your way to any of the squares marked with a symbol. You may travel over each square as often as you like.

❄	8	6	5	7	7	2	4	6	2	❄
8	3	9	6	3	8	3	9	5	6	4
4	9	5	3	6	9	9	4	6	8	9
6	8	3	9	7	3	4	4	2	5	4
2	5	8	3	4	9	3	2	3	9	1
4	2	4	6	9	3	5	8	3	9	2
9	5	6	2	6	7	9	2	6	8	2
6	3	8	4	7	4	8	4	9	9	6
5	8	5	4	4	7	5	9	4	8	4
2	7	4	2	5	7	2	9	2	8	6
❄	4	9	4	4	2	7	5	3	1	❄

Win Sum–Lose Sum

Begin at 2 and move in any direction (including diagonally) to an adjacent square. Add the number in this square to that in the square you just left. The sum of those two numbers will be a number in an adjacent square (2+4=6, etc.). Move there. Repeat this process until you reach 100.

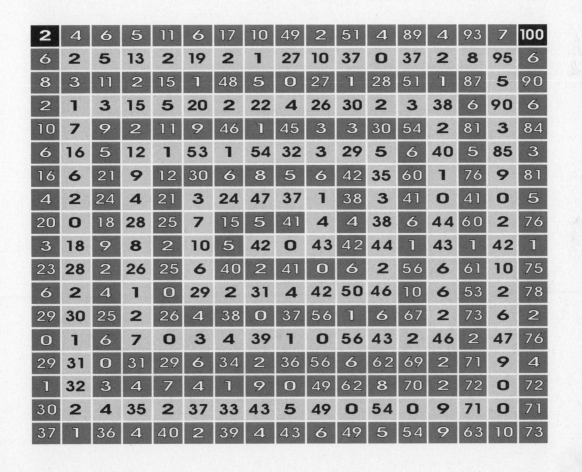

Geometry

Simple geometric shapes: hexagons, squares, triangles, and hex-nuts! Easy stuff for those geo-types. But these Lateral Logic Mazes add just a touch of madness to the proceedings. Maybe it's a hex or maybe it's a square. Or maybe someone's put a hex on a square. It's obviously a triangle, but where did the extra piece come from?

Don't be intimidated by a circle that has to become a square or things like that. Before you challenge each circle to a duel, try the maze as it is and see where it takes you. You might be surprised.

Once you overcome these puzzles, the rest of the book will be a breeze.

Hex or Square

The pieces below fit together as either a square or a hexagon. Make your decision and build one of the options. Now solve the maze as the path winds over and under itself.

Square Circles

Begin with the S and work your way through the maze horizontally and vertically (NOT diagonally), alternating from square to circle. Try to reach the C. By the way, one circle should be a square. Change it to win.

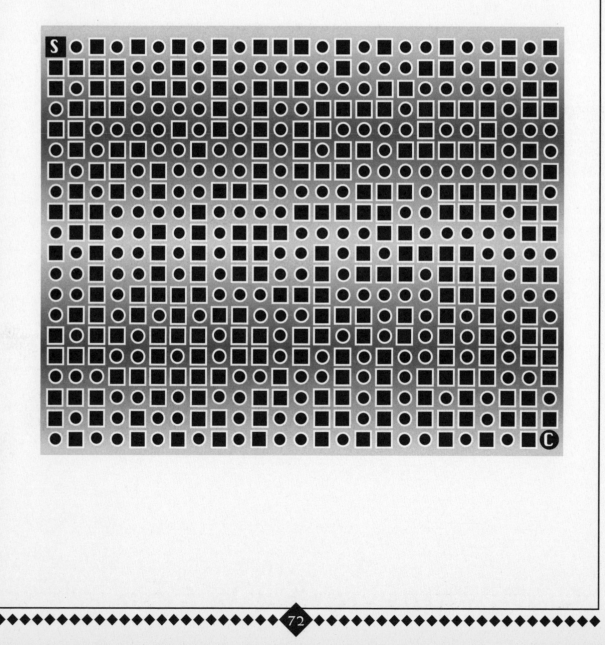

Three Nuts

🐿 The path shown on the puzzle begins at the 1, and touches all the nuts only once. Find a path that begins at 2 and also touches all the nuts. Now find another that begins at 3. It's not as easy as it looks.

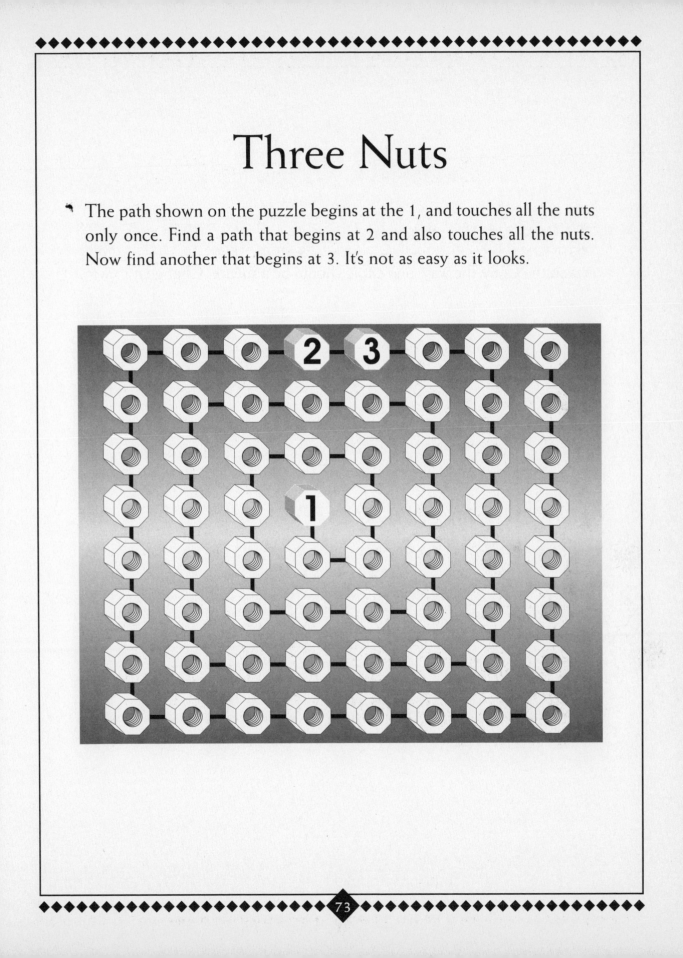

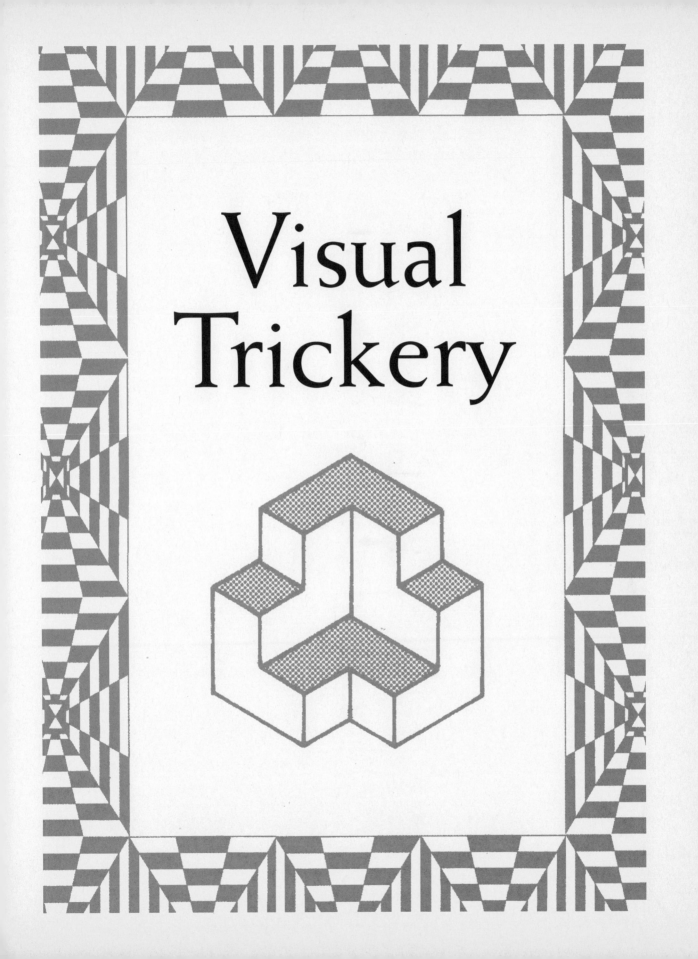

Visual
Trickery

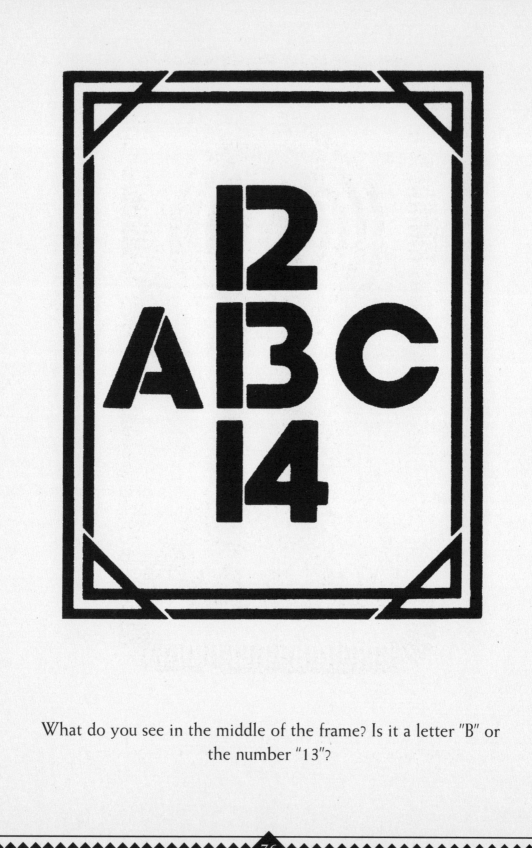

What do you see in the middle of the frame? Is it a letter "B" or the number "13"?

Rotate the page in a circular motion. What happens?

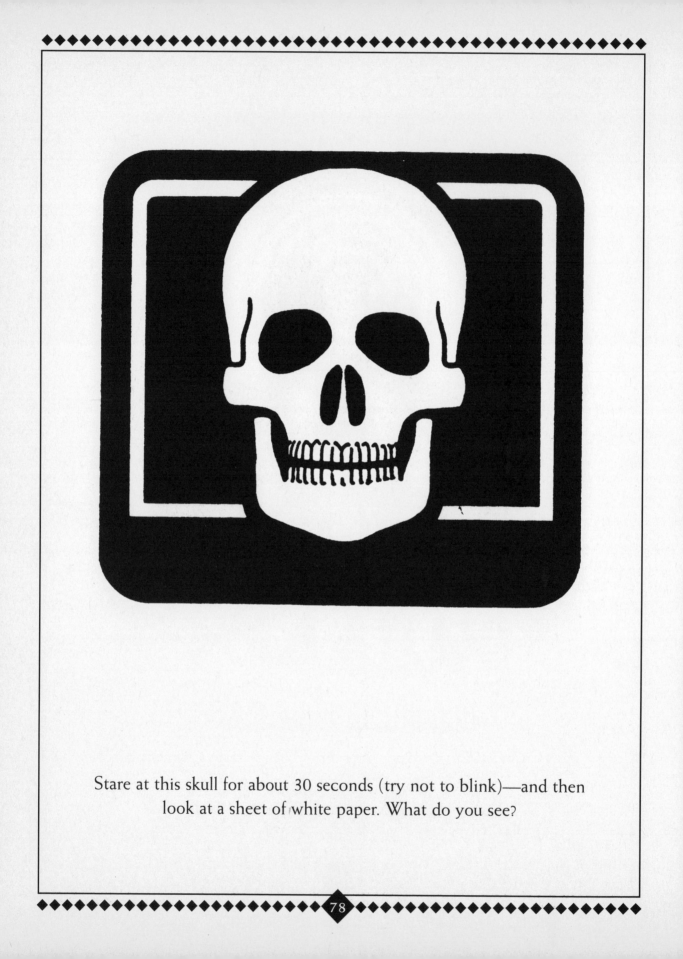

Stare at this skull for about 30 seconds (try not to blink)—and then look at a sheet of white paper. What do you see?

What is mysterious about these donkeys?

Are these stacks of banknotes sloping downwards to the right, or are they pointing down to the left?

At first glance, we see a pig. But where is the farmer?

What are you looking at—the inside of a tunnel—or the
top of a mountain?

Stare at the center of the illustration. Then slowly bring the page close to your face. What happens?

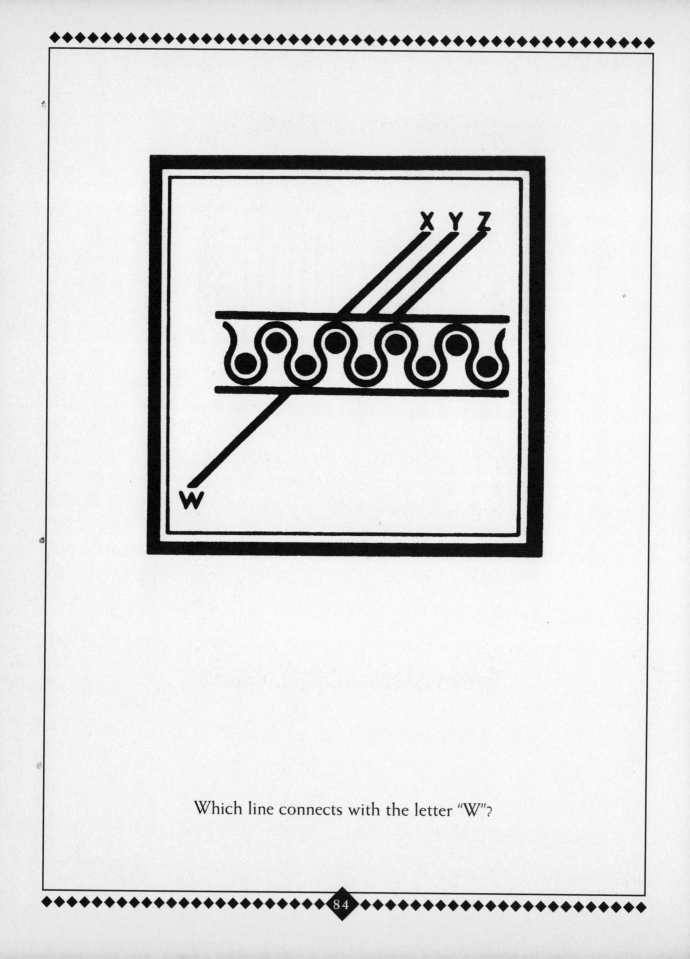

Which line connects with the letter "W"?

How many candles are there?

The famous magician Dunninger used this design as a logo. Do you notice something odd about his features?

Death

Is there life after death?

Is the zebra white with black stripes or black with white stripes?

This is Garibaldi. Turn him upside down
and who does he become?

What do you see—black wine glasses or white vases?

Would you describe the back wheel of this cycle as a circle?

Can you spot the dog? What is he an example of?

Can you decipher the Mandarin's scroll?
Clue: It has to do with playing cards.

What's wrong with these fish?

Which way are the tubes facing?

Do you notice anything unusual about this apple core?

This elephant is weird. Why?

Is this clown balancing on a white ball with a black pattern or on a black ball with a white pattern?

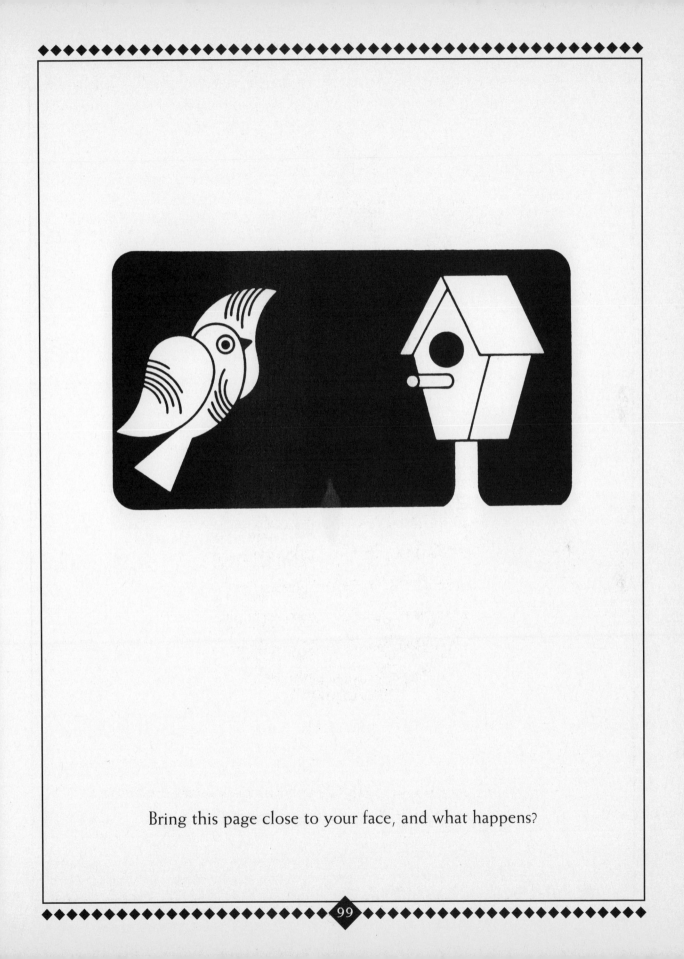

Bring this page close to your face, and what happens?

You can make this distorted checkerboard perfectly square
without touching it. How?

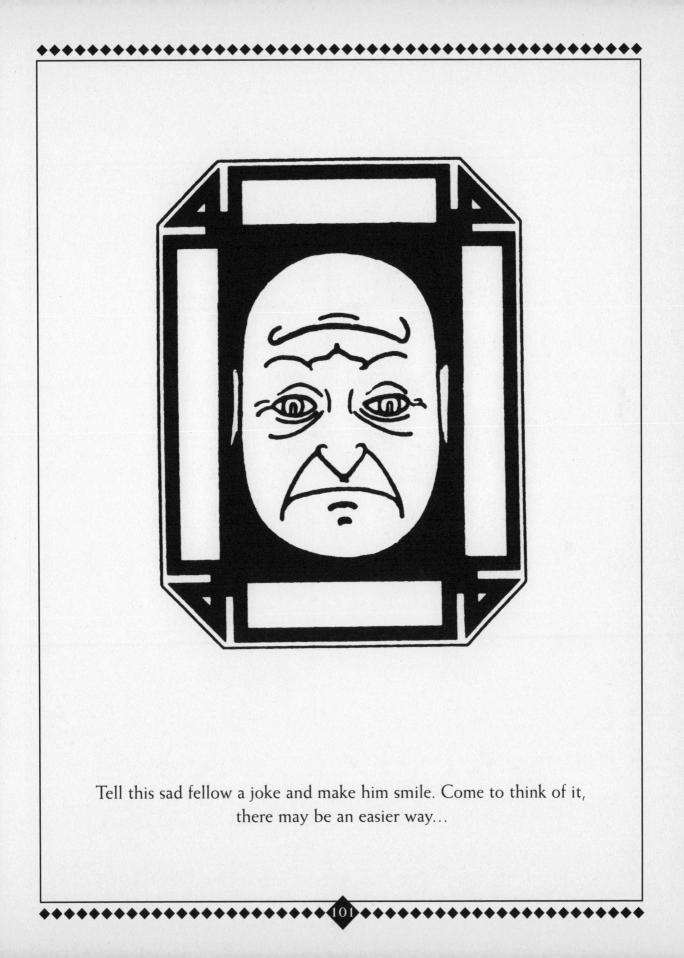

Tell this sad fellow a joke and make him smile. Come to think of it,
there may be an easier way…

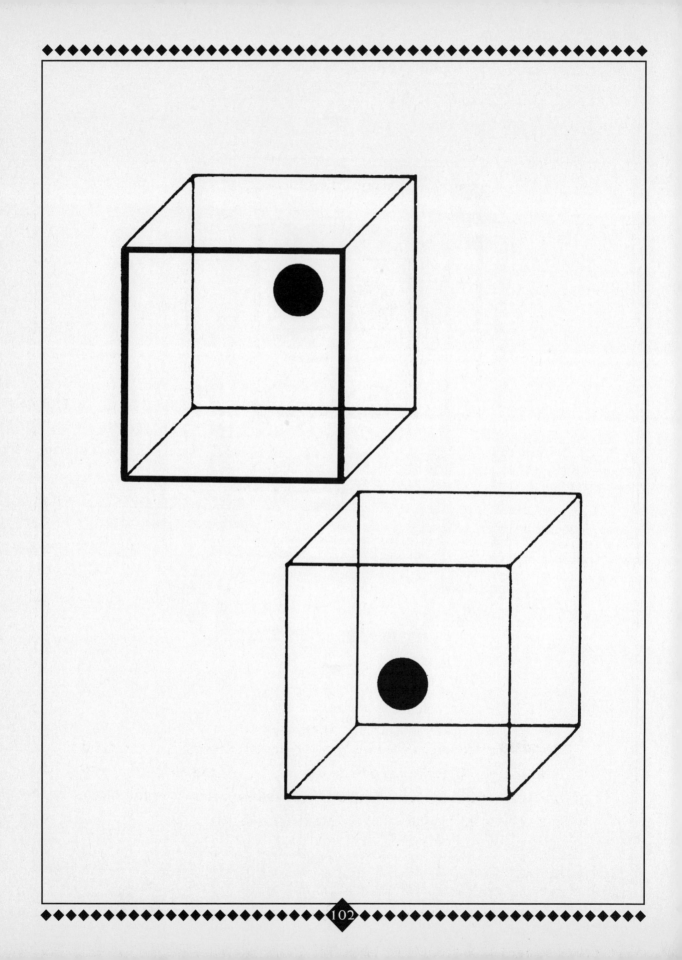

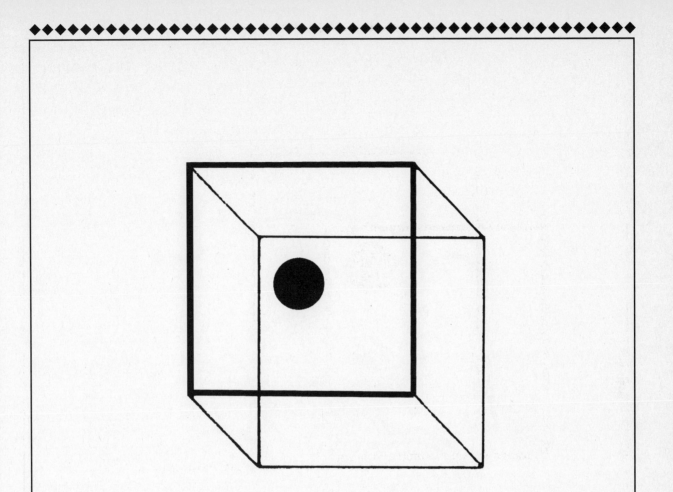

Do you see the areas bounded by the darker lines as the outside of the transparent cubes? Keep looking, and the bounded area will become the inner surface of a cube tilted a different way. Are the black spots on the front or rear face, or inside the cubes?

Rotate this page in a counterclockwise direction. What happens?

Which of the two small squares is larger?

Is Side "A" of this picture high or is Side "B"?

What do you see in this picture?

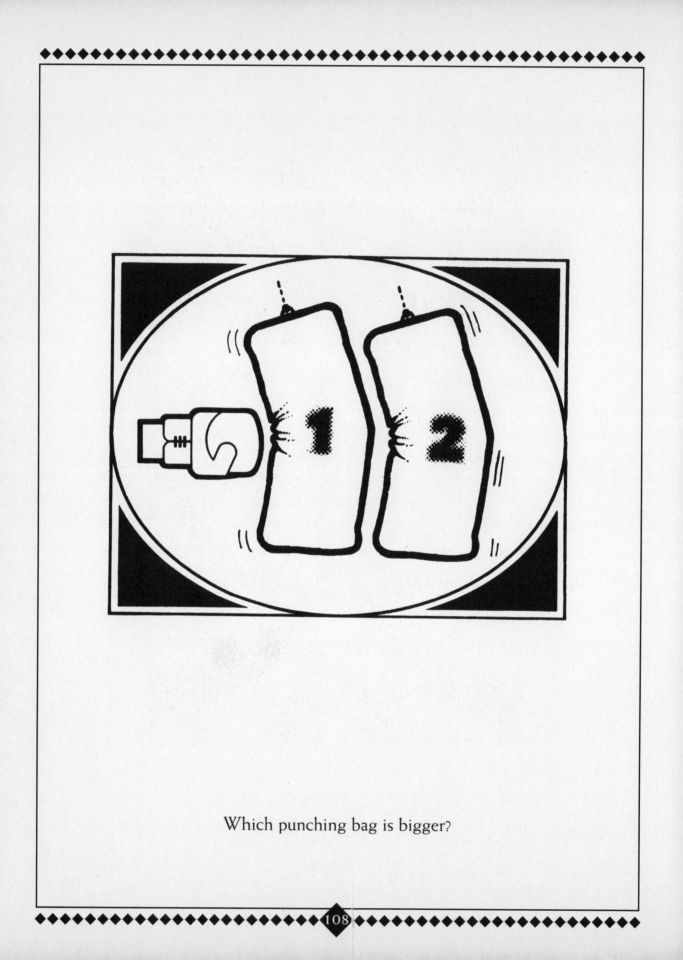

Which punching bag is bigger?

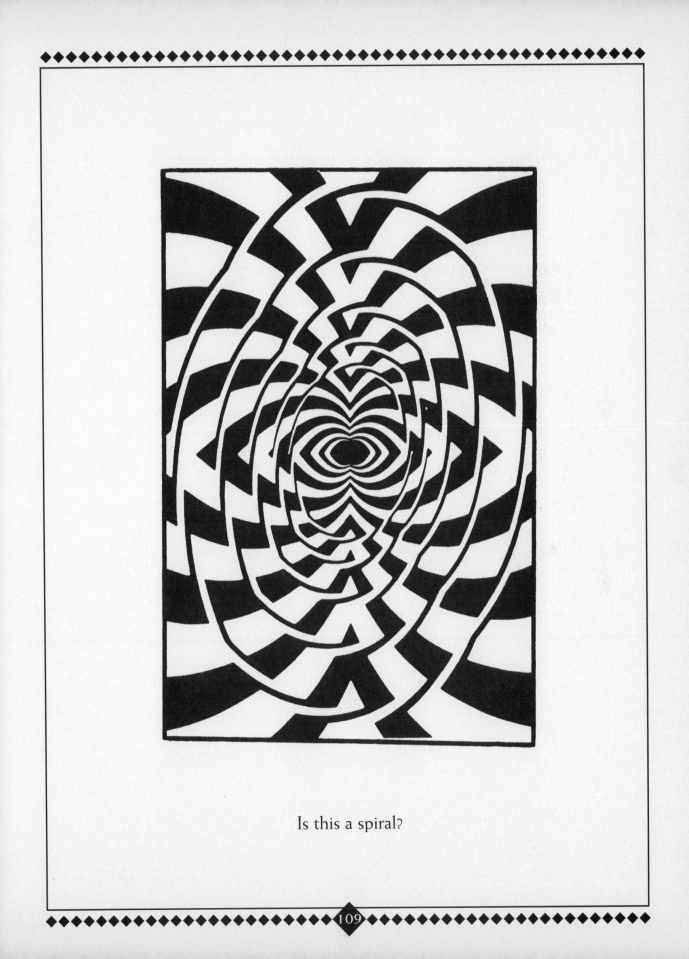

Is this a spiral?

What's the matter with these cubes?

What do you see in this picture—black arrows or white arrows?

Why do the fish in this illustration seem to swim in
one direction and then in the other?

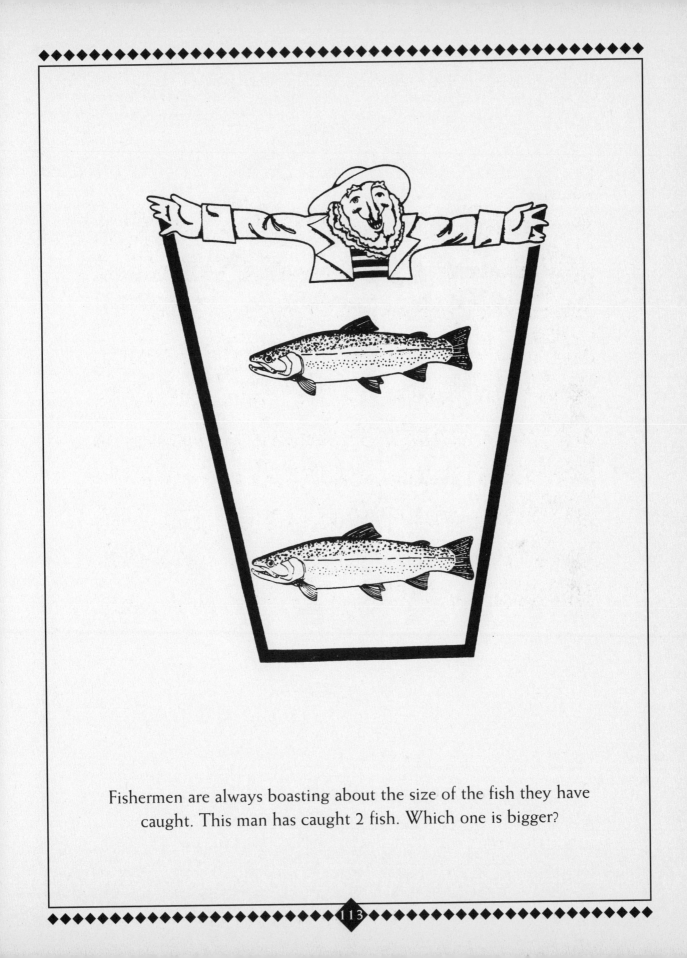

Fishermen are always boasting about the size of the fish they have caught. This man has caught 2 fish. Which one is bigger?

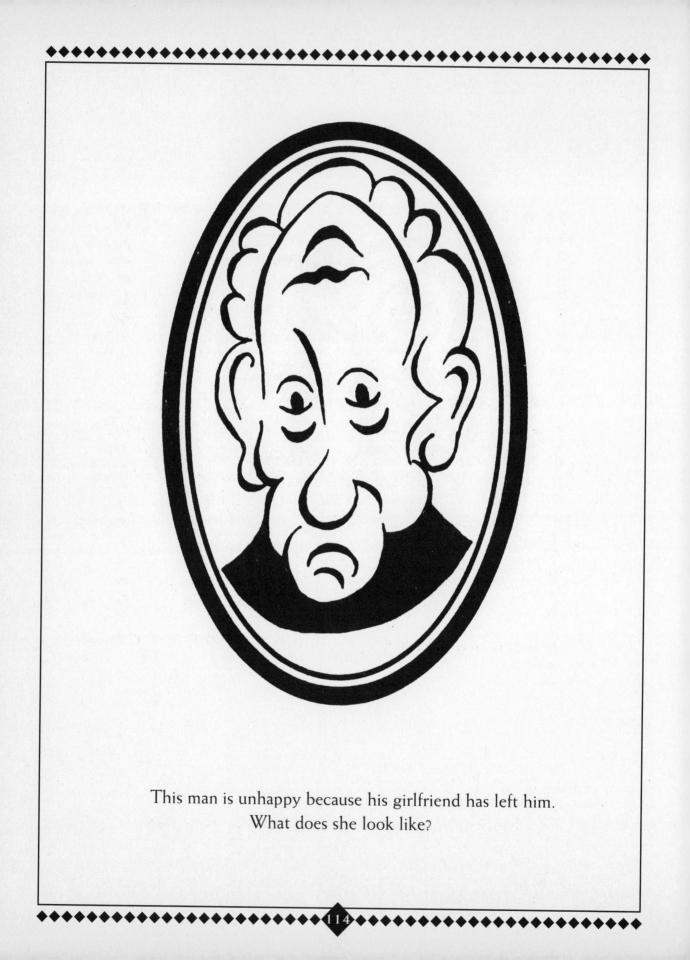

This man is unhappy because his girlfriend has left him.
What does she look like?

What happens when you rotate this page in a circular motion?

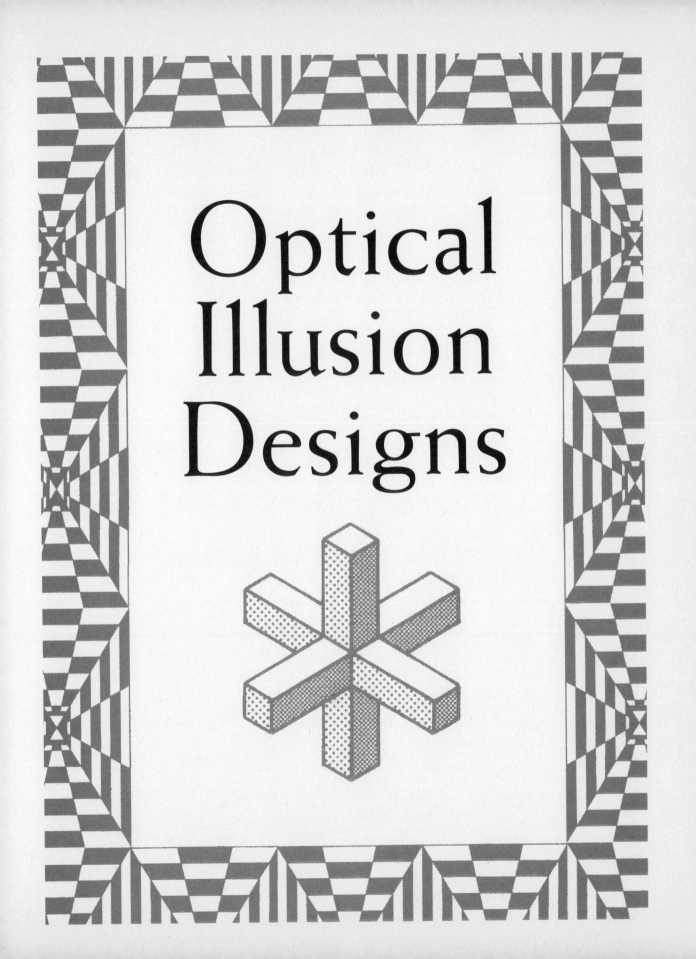

Optical Illusion Designs

Shimmering Squares

The shimmering effect you see below is caused by optical distortion. This illusion is unusual because all the lines in it are sloped either forward at 45° or backward at 135°. To see why this helps make the illusion more interesting, try the following experiment.

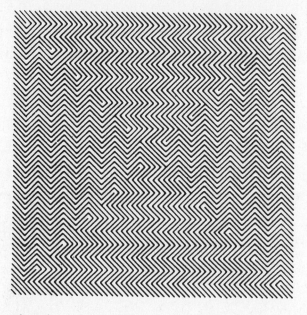

Concentrate hard on one of the rows of lines that are sloped at 45°—like the bottom edge of a square. You'll find that all the squares formed by lines sloped at 45° appear steady, while the ones formed by lines sloping backwards at 135° look blurry and faint and seem to shimmer.

Then concentrate on a row of lines sloped at 135° and you'll see that all the squares formed with lines sloped at 45° will look blurry and faint and seem to shimmer.

This effect occurs because your eyes cannot focus on all of the illusion at once. The parts of the illusion that you do focus on will appear clear, while the parts of the illusion that are out of focus will look blurry.

All Square

This optical illusion is especially puzzling. If you study it closely, the ovals in the middle first seem to bulge out and then they seem to recede.

The reason why they change is that when your eyes scan the design from left to right, the position of the ovals suggests to your brain that the ovals are popping out. But then your eyes go back over the picture. With so many different ways to scan the illusion—and no clues to which way is "right"—you may see the ovals recede, or do any number of interesting tricks.

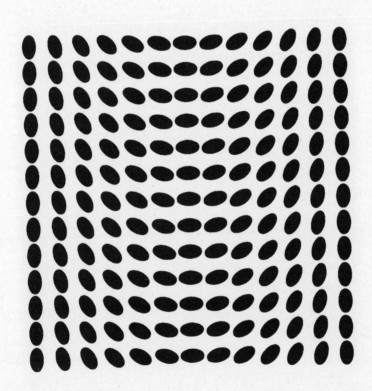

Making Waves

When you stare at this optical illusion for a while, the curved lines seem to form the crests and valleys of waves. They may even seem to move a little. If you stare some more, until your eyes get tired, you may also see phantom lines of color, especially in bright light, where the curved lines run parallel to each other—between the valleys and crests of the waves.

The restless motion of the waves in this illusion is caused by optical distortion.

Tricky Tiles

What makes this design vibrate? Right, it's optical distortion again! The repetition of the same design on each tile helps to make this illusion even more effective.

Jester

If you look at this circular checkerboard closely, it will seem to pulsate and shimmer. You may also see the black-and-white patches link up to form the petals of a flower.

The shimmering that you see is caused by optical distortion. But the petals formed by your brain are an example of another phenomenon called "good continuation." It happens because your brain is trying to make sense out of what it sees. It seeks out shapes or patterns that it recognizes. Sometimes it works so hard and so cleverly that it imagines an object that isn't really there. And then we have an optical illusion.

Networking

In this neat illusion, tiny white dots appear to join together to form phantom white crosses. This is another example of your brain trying to make sense of the visual information it is receiving—good continuation.

But there is another interesting phenomenon at work here. You can also see tiny gray dots in the center of the black crosses. Why? Special cells in your visual system respond strongly to small patches of light and dark. If a small light patch is surrounded by more light, these cells will not respond so strongly to the small patch of light in the middle. If a small dark patch is surrounded by more darkness, these cells will not respond so strongly to the small patch of dark in the middle.

So in the case of the black crosses, your visual system does not respond fully to the middle of them, and you see them as gray instead.

It doesn't have to be this way, though. You can force your eyes and brain not to "overlook" the midpoint of the crosses. If you focus your eyes and attention fully upon one cross at a time, you will be able to see it as an ordinary black cross.

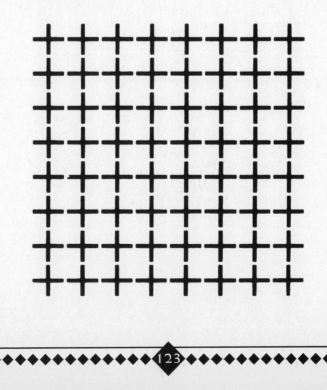

Zinnia

When you look at this illusion, you may see some gray or white spots at the points where the black lines meet. This is caused by your eyes' response to dark and light, as in "Networking."

And, if you go on studying this design, you may also see that these imaginary dots "link up" to form a series of circles that radiate out from the middle of the illusion. This is another example of good continuation.

Lattice

Here is an example of the role that contrast plays in your perceptions. Although there are only two colors used in this design—black and white—the tiny white dots in the middle, where the black lines intersect, seem brighter and whiter than the larger white squares. This is because the tiny white squares are more completely surrounded by the black lines than the larger white squares.

Square's Square

This illusion may remind you of "Shimmering Squares" (page 118), in which lines drawn at different angles confuse the brain. The squares here that have been drawn on the background pattern may look as if they have been bent, but in actual fact they are perfectly straight!

This is an example of the "Zollner effect." It shows how straight lines appear to bend if they intersect with or are seen against a background of curved lines or lines drawn at different angles. This strange effect occurs because your eyes and brain work together to try to make the straight lines fit into the background pattern.

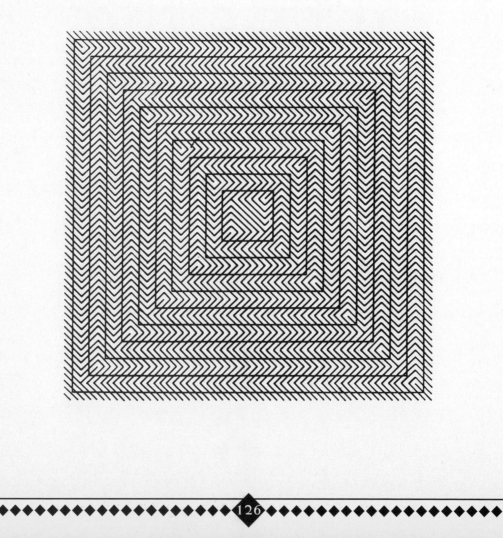

Spiral Square-Case

The squares in the foreground look as if they are bent, right? Well, they do look that way. But this is another example of the Zollner effect. If you hold a ruler up alongside them, you'll see that the lines in the square are just as straight as they can be. It's only the curves of the spiral background that make the square seem bent.

Squashed Circles

You can see all sorts of different effects when you look at this illusion. You may see flickering spokes radiating out from the central circle— turn the page from side to side to accentuate this effect. You can also view the central and smallest circle in two ways: as the top of a cone or as the end of a funnel.

The flickering spokes are a result of optical distortion.

Seasick Circle

If you watch this drawing while you turn the book around in a circle, you will be able to see a series of spirals moving up and down in three dimensions.

This is what's called a "stereokinetic effect." It's the result of a complex series of interactions between your eyes and your brain.

When this design rotates, the images sent to your brain are constantly changing. Because each circle is drawn with lines that vary in thickness, there is no stable point in the illusion for you to focus on. This is confusing to your brain, which likes to make orderly patterns out of what it sees. So your brain looks for another pattern and sees that some of the curved lines seem to link up to form a spiral. As the curves that form the spiral rotate and change position, each of your eyes simultaneously sends your brain a slightly different image. When your brain puts this all together, it decides that it must be seeing a spiral moving up and down.

The Temple

This illusion combines two effects. It is a reversing figure. One way to look at it is as a pyramid viewed from above, with the smallest square forming the top. The other is as a passageway leading towards a tiny square door. If you look steadily at this illusion, you will probably see it flash between these two images.

It is also an example of optical distortion, because of the way it seems to shimmer.

The Escalator

When you look closely at this optical illusion, you may get the impression that the horizontal panels are moving with a tiny jerking motion. The central panel may also seem unexpectedly bright. The reason that the "Escalator" appears to move is that, no matter how hard you try, you can't keep your eyes perfectly still, and as they move about, so do the images in the illusion.

Escalator Experiment

To fully appreciate this illusion, ask a teacher or librarian to photocopy this picture onto a plastic film to make a transparency. Place the transparency over the illusion and move it from side to side. You will experience the incredible "moiré effect" when the two patterns are superimposed.

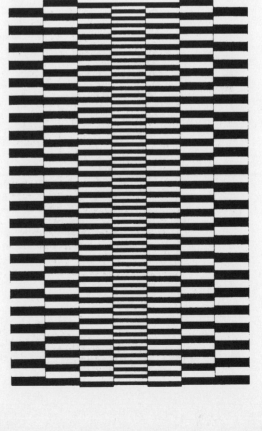

You have undoubtedly observed the moiré effect before. It is in the patterns you see when two lace curtains overlap. It is produced where the thicker strands of the lace cross over each other to form a pattern.

You can also create a moiré effect using two combs. Hold them up to the light and slowly rotate one of the combs against the other. You will see a series of moiré fringes or bands appearing and disappearing.

Moiré Grating

This is one of the simplest types of moiré pattern, one formed by two identical gratings. The pattern you see is so strong that it is very difficult to see the path of each individual straight line. Try tracing the path of any straight black line with your finger and you'll see.

The Eternal Staircase

Can you figure out which corner of the staircase is the highest? Probably not. Because this is not a real staircase—it's an "impossible figure." The drawing works because your brain recognizes it as three-dimensional. And a good deal of it is a realistic depiction. The first time you glance at it, the steps in "The Eternal Staircase" look quite

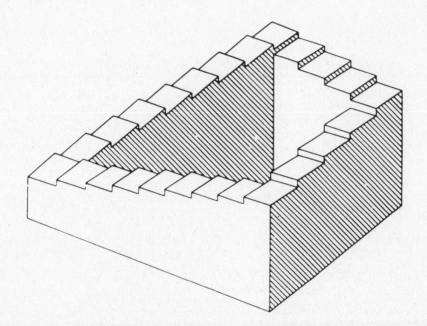

logical. It is only when you look at the drawing closely that you see that the entire structure is impossible.

"The Eternal Staircase" was first created by Lionel S. Penrose, a geneticist, and his son Roger. It later became known through the work of Maurits Escher, an artist who worked in the early part of the 20th century. Escher used many impossible figures such as this in his art, creating extremely odd paintings.

The Impossible Triangle

Even if you were an expert carpenter, you'd never be able to construct this figure. Each of the three joints in the triangle is drawn with great accuracy. But the rods connecting them are not!

The fascinating thing about these illusions is that your brain is so convinced they are drawings of three-dimensional figures, that it is almost impossible to see them as the flat outline drawings they are.

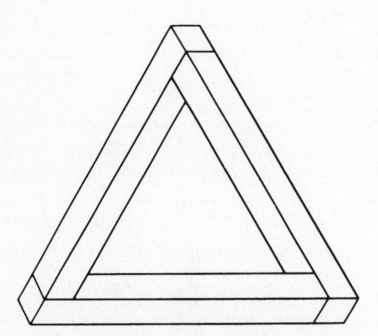

Chrysanthemum

When you look at this design, you get the impression that it is not flat, but three-dimensional. Some parts of the illusion appear higher and some lower, which gives the impression of depth. However, if you look at the curved lines that define the bumps and hollows of the flower, you will find a curious situation. Look at the curve that defines the outer edge of the flower, for instance, and follow it right around in a circle. You will see that in some places the curved lines seem to define a hump—and at others a hollow. This object could not exist in three dimensions. "Chrysanthemum" is another example of an impossible figure.

It also shimmers—so it is also a case of optical distortion.

More Mazes

Blow Out

This is a basic 3-dimensional maze. The pipes are channel tubes that float in perspective over and under each other. Enter the maze at the WHITE ball and crawl through the tubes to the BLACK ball. There is more than one solution, but if you can't find any, a solution can be found in the back of the book, on page 370.

Structure Impossible

Work your way through the construction from globe to globe. On your way, try to travel through each BLACK cube only once. You may not retrace your path but you MAY return to the starting cube as often as you like.

The Warehouse

Enter the warehouse and walk to the back exit. You may open only FIVE doors on your journey.

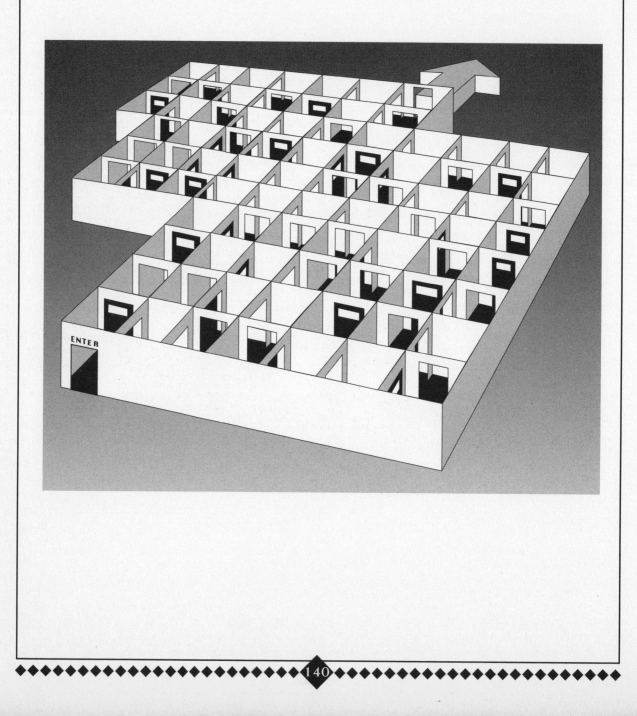

The Cubic Hotel

Your room is the BLACK cubicle in the east wing of the hotel. To save money, the developers have eliminated the hallways from this hostelry. Enter the correct entry door and find the way to your room.

Cube Madness

The nine cubes in this puzzle have 15 sides showing. Some of the sides are in the correct place and some are not. To solve this maze, rearrange the incorrect sides and then travel from arrow to arrow as the path winds over and under itself.

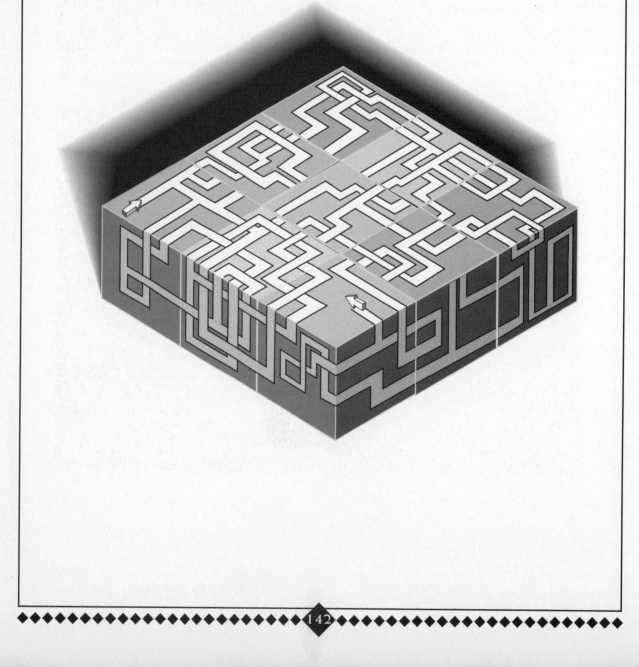

Round and Round

If you start from the central globe, only one of the four mazes leads to an OUT arrow. Using just your eyes, can you discover the correct maze?

Pipe Down

Enter at the WHITE ball and travel through the pipes, touching ALL the balls once. You may not retrace your steps as you return to the WHITE ball. You may add TWO connecting pipes to solve this puzzle if you need them.

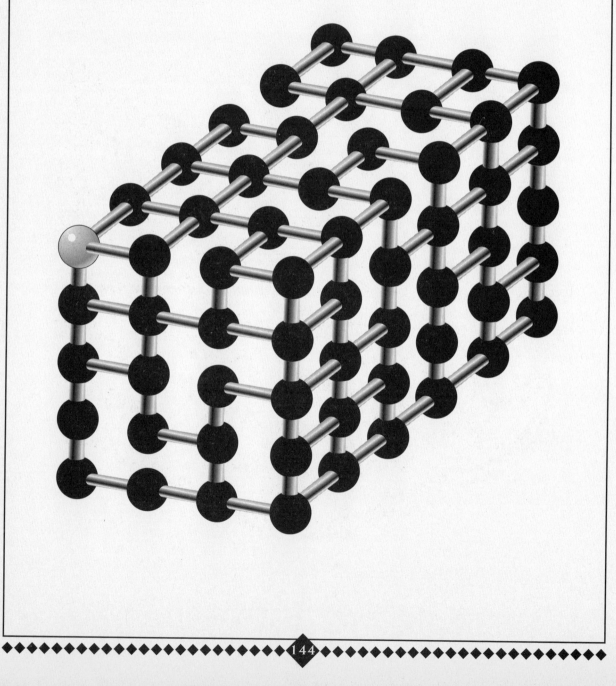

Ball, Pyramid & Cube

From the IN arrow find a path that touches all the objects only once before exiting. You must alternate between objects (ball—pyramid—cube, or ball—cube—pyramid) as you travel along your route. You must maintain the same sequence you began with throughout your journey.

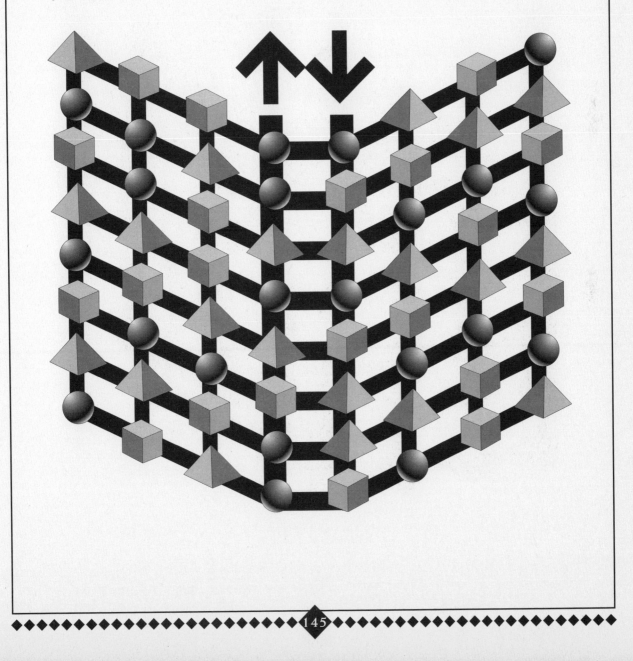

In and Out

Starting at the BLACK pyramid, crawl through the pipes, touching all the solid objects in sequence (pyramid—ball—cube or pyramid—cube—ball). Then exit at the BLACK pyramid. You may not retrace your steps or touch any object more than once. You must also maintain the sequence you began with.

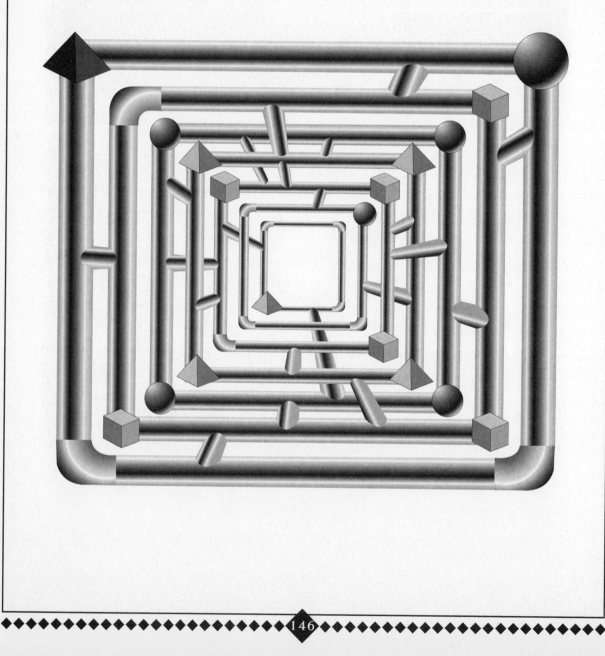

Ending Well

Follow the arrows and touch every space except the center. Be careful, however. Two arrows are facing in the WRONG direction.

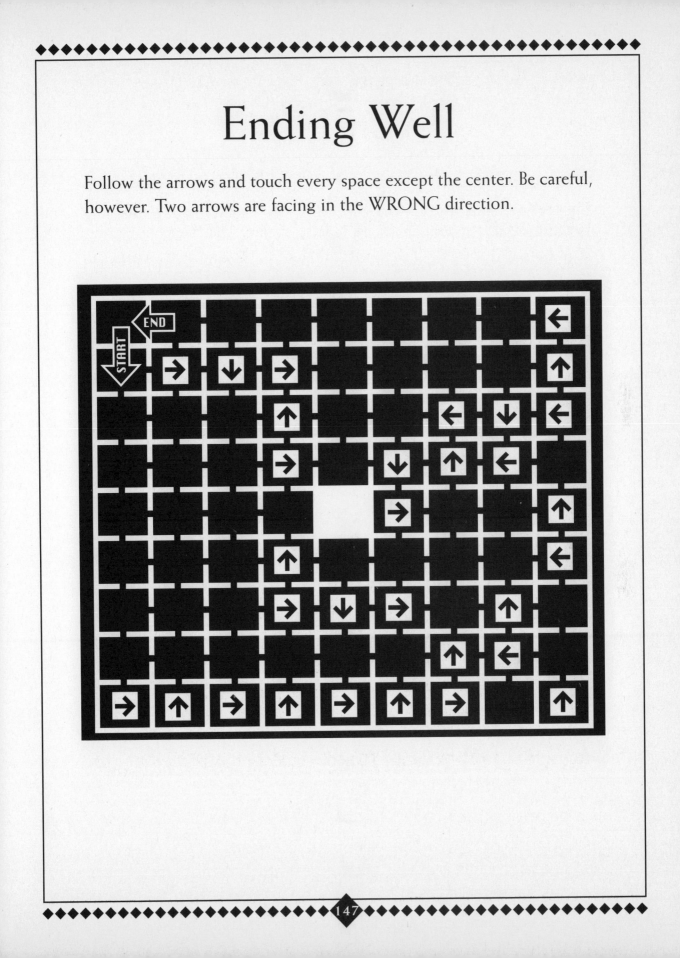

Clear Logic

Follow the path from the IN arrow to the OUT arrow. The path is etched on clear glass so you can follow it around the solid shape. The path flows over and under itself.

Jump Ball

Voyage into the maze by starting at the BLACK ball. When you reach a GRAY ball, jump to any other GRAY ball and continue through the pipes to the next GRAY ball. Jump again and continue the process until you touch all the GRAY balls; then exit at the WHITE ball. You may not retrace your path or touch any GRAY ball more than once.

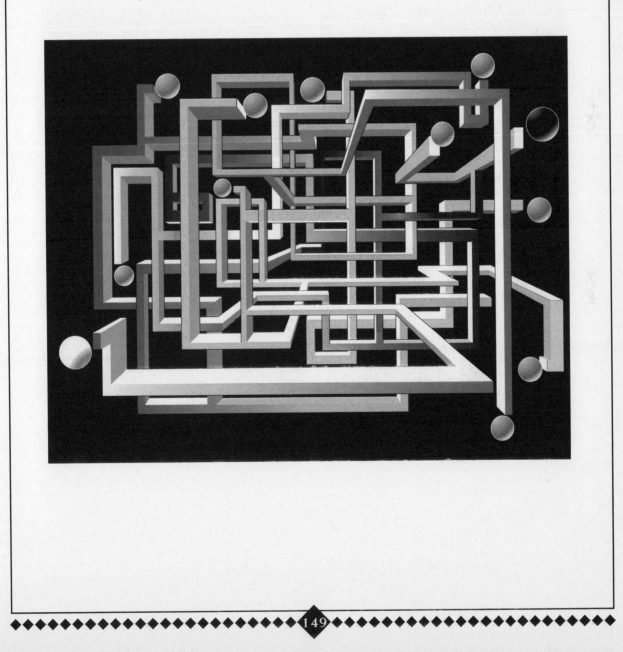

The Black and White Ball

Enter the maze at any ball and travel to an opposite (WHITE to BLACK or BLACK to WHITE) ball. Then jump from the ball you have just reached to a ball of opposite value. Continue through the pipes, repeating the first sequence until you have touched all eight balls. Then exit at the OUT arrow. You may retrace your path as often as you like. There are many solutions to this maze, and you can find one solution on page 251.

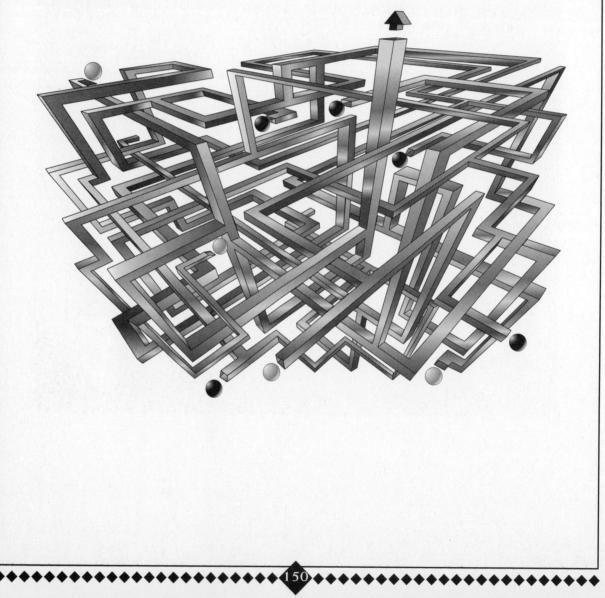

Way Out

Find the IN arrow and enter the maze on a search for fourteen balls. When you reach a ball, you must jump to another ball of opposite value (BLACK to WHITE or WHITE to BLACK), then enter the pipe and repeat the process. You must touch ALL the balls in the prior sequence before exiting at the OUT arrow. You may not travel over any path or touch any ball more than once.

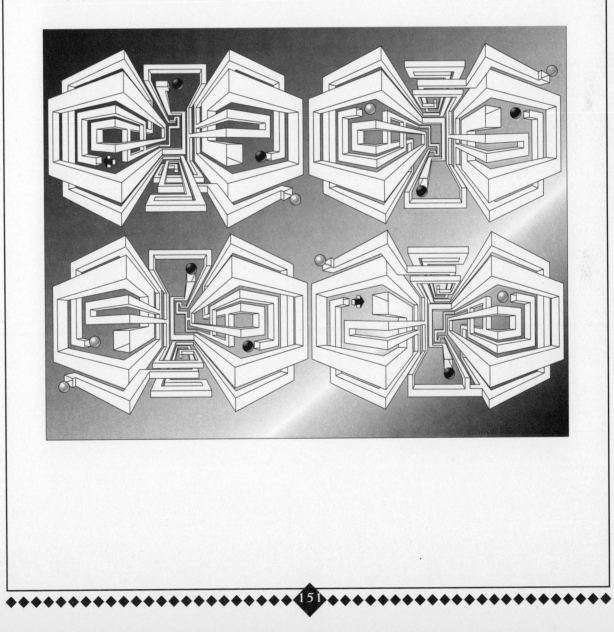

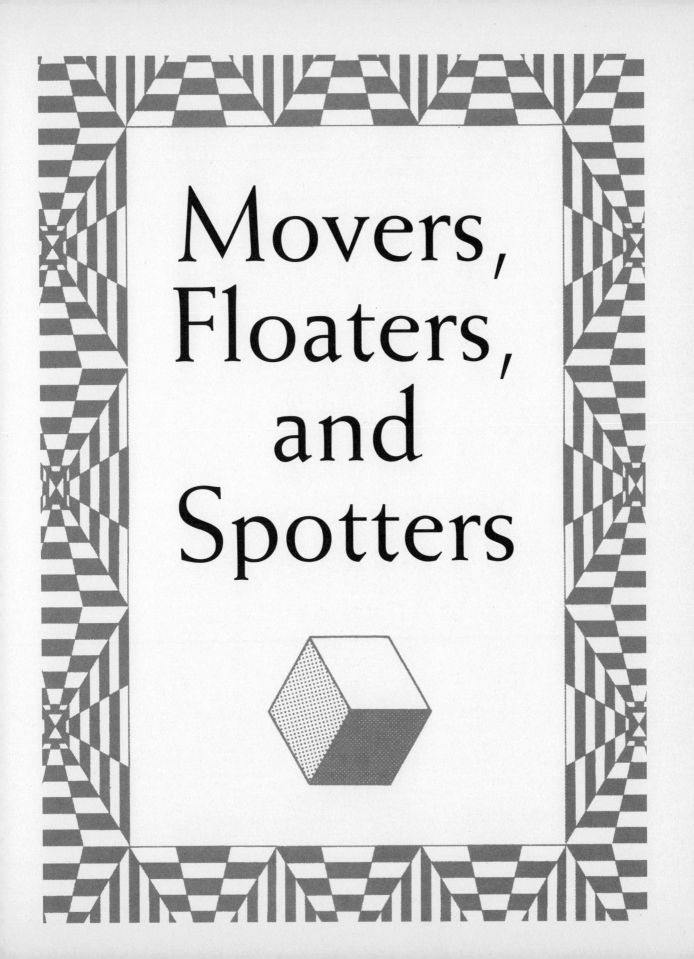

Movers, Floaters, and Spotters

An optical illusion is something that looks different from what it really is. Some optical illusions, like the ones in this book, look different because they seem to move.

Some optical illusions appear because we have two eyes, while others are the result of our brain remembering one thing while our eyes are seeing another. Still other illusions happen because we think we see one thing when we actually see something else.

Here are a few optical illusions that result from seeing things with two eyes.

The Floating Finger

Hold your hands in front of your face at eye level, about 15 inches away from your eyes. Illus. 1 shows how. Keep the tips of your index fingers about 1 inch apart.

Illus. 1

Focus on a wall several feet behind your fingers. Almost at once you will see something strange. Between the tips of your fingers is a tiny, disembodied finger floating in space. Strangest of all is the fact that this little finger has two tips, one at either end.

Slowly move your hands closer to your face. Keep the tips of your fingers the same distance apart. The nearer your hands come to your face the longer the little floating finger becomes.

Pull your hands away from your face and the little two-ended finger gets shorter and shorter. Illus. 2 shows this illusion.

Illus. 2

Now, focus your eyes on your fingers instead of the wall. Just like that, the floating finger vanishes.

When your fingers move closer to your face the space between them enters a "blind spot" (you'll find out more about these on page 160). Rather than go blind, your brain knows what should be there and fills the spot with what your eyes *do* see. In this case, your eyes see the ends of your fingers and your brain uses this sight to fill the blind spot. That's why you see the floating finger even though it's not there, and why it disappears when you look at your actual fingers.

The Jumping Finger

Hold up the index finger of either hand and shut one eye. Move your index finger until it points directly at some object or is directly under some object. The illustration below shows how.

Close one eye and don't move your finger. Did your finger jump? Try closing your other eye. It jumped back again!

Of course your finger did not move (at least it's not supposed to). So what happened? Because your eyes are several inches apart, each one actually sees a slightly different picture. Your brain puts the two pictures together to tell how far an object is.

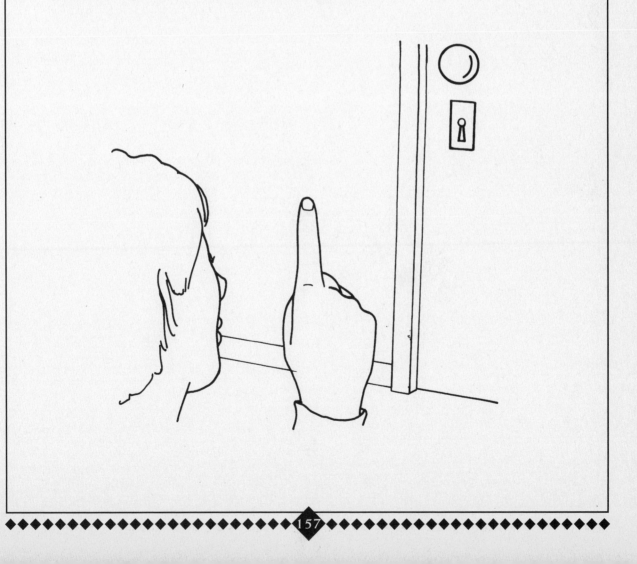

The Bouncing Ring

Open up both your eyes and form your thumb and forefinger into a ring like the one shown below.

Hold this ring out at arm's length. Move it around until you find something across the room which fits nicely into the ring. Focus your eyes on the object inside the ring.

Close one eye. Is the object still inside the ring? Depending on which eye you closed, the ring may stay still or bounce back.

Without moving your ring, close your open eye and open your closed eye. Now what do you see inside your ring?

With one eye open the object lines up inside the ring, but with your other eye open the object bounces away. Why?

When you see things with both eyes, one eye has more control than the other. The eye that has more control is sometimes called the "dominant eye." When you close your dominant eye, the picture changes.

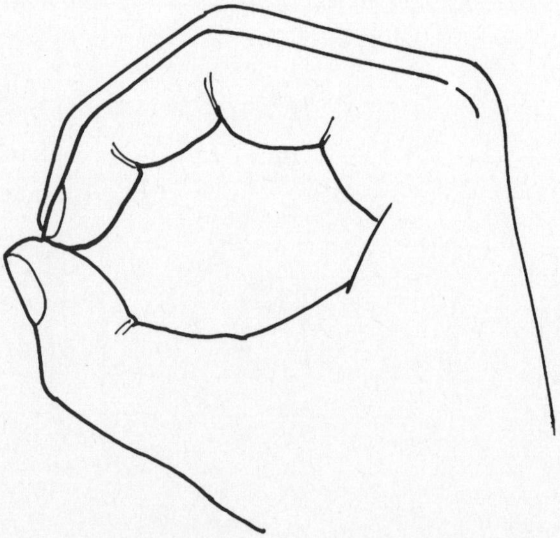

Growing New Fingers

While you're holding hands and fingers up, here's another moving illusion. Hold your index finger at arm's length, and keep both eyes open. Look at some object across the room that is in line with your extended finger. The illustration below shows how.

Focus on the object across the room and now you've got an extra finger.

Now focus on your finger. You see *two* objects instead of one!

Obviously, you did not grow an extra finger, nor did the object across the room suddenly double. What you did was see two different pictures with each eye.

Blind Spots

Do we always see—all the time—unless our eyes are closed or we are in a dark place? Maybe, maybe not.

Hold the illustration at the bottom of this page about 15 inches in front of your face. Close your left eye and look directly at the airplane with your right (open) eye.

Slowly move the book closer to you, looking *directly* at the airplane with your right eye. Move the book closer and farther until something strange happens. Suddenly the rocket will disappear!

No, it didn't leap off the page, or move somewhere else. What happened was it got lost in your blind spot. Don't worry, everyone has one in each eye, so you're not going blind.

Now close your right eye and open your left. With the left eye stare directly at the rocket and move the illustration closer and farther until suddenly the airplane disappears. The plane moved into the blind spot in your left eye.

Viewing the illustration with only one eye at a time you get a chance to locate your blind spot. When you are looking at things with both eyes this tiny blind spot causes no problem. What one eye does not see the other does.

Hole in Your Hand

Do you have a hole in the palm of your hand? No? Don't be too sure.

Roll a sheet of notebook paper into a hollow tube about 1 inch across. Hold the tube to keep it from unrolling or use a strip of cellophane tape to fasten the loose edge down. This is up to you.

Hold the tube up to one eye as shown below. Keep your other eye open.

Don't poke yourself in the eye with the tube.

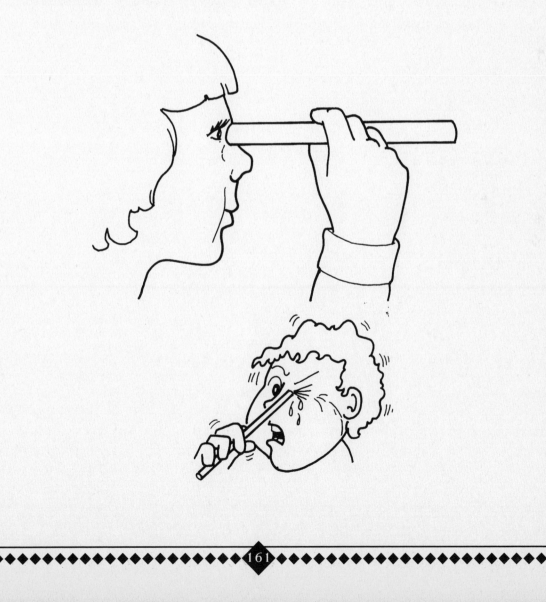

Locate something across the room that is small enough to be seen through the hollow tube. The object should be 12 to 15 feet away. Keep both eyes open, and look at the object through the tube.

Now bring your other hand up in front of the eye not looking through the paper tube. (The illustration below shows how to do this.) Suddenly you develop a round hole in the palm of your hand! And you're looking at the object through that round hole!

Naturally, this is just an optical illusion. This is one more time when seeing with both eyes makes you think things are not as they actually are.

Now is as good a time as any to mention the fact that you will get lots more fun out of this book when you share the illusions with others. See how each moving optical illusion works. Then share it with friends and family.

The Traveling Rectangle

Sometimes your brain remembers an image even after you no longer see it. This is another optical illusion that moves from place to place.

Stare directly at the black rectangle in the illustration below. Count to 30 as you stare. Try to blink as little as possible, but don't worry if a blink or two slips in. It won't spoil anything.

After staring for a count of 30, look up from the page. Now stare right at a dark wall or some other dark surface. Keep staring. What appears?

You know the rectangle didn't move off the page, but there it is! Even stranger than the fact that the rectangle moved to the wall is the fact that the one on the wall is light or even white instead of black like the one in the book!

This is called *afterimage*. Afterimage is responsible for many moving optical illusions. Some of them trick us into thinking we see colors that are different from those we really see. But more about that later.

Lines and Lines

Take a quick look the illustration below. As you can see there are two slanting lines that meet two parallel lines.

So what is so special about this? The special thing is that your eyes and mind have created an optical illusion.

Let's see if a little moving around will clear up the illusion. Take a piece of paper with a straight edge. Place the straight edge along the two slanted lines.

This is one of those times when just a little movement does an amazing thing to an optical illusion.

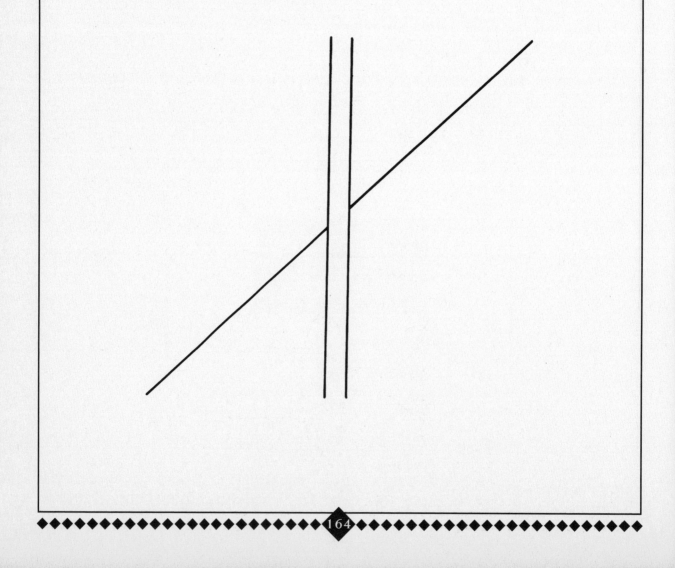

Three Arrows

For this illusion you need a glass that you can see through.

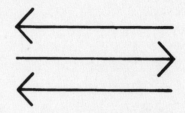

First, fill the glass part-way with water, then look at these three arrows. Copy these arrows onto a sheet of notebook paper. Place the arrows low on the page so that you can easily slip the paper behind the filled part of the glass.

Hold the paper with the arrows a few inches behind the water glass. Look through the glass of water at the arrows. Move the paper back and forth until the arrows come into focus.

The arrows get longer and shorter, because the curved water acts like a magnifying glass.

But what else do you see? Check the arrows you drew. The outside arrows point to the right, and the inside one points to the left. Now look through the water again.

Of course, the arrows didn't reverse themselves. They look this way because you're looking through the water rather than the air. The water does the same thing to the arrows that a convex lens does. A convex lens is the type with the bulged-out sides, and it reverses whatever you're looking at. The illustration below shows how the light enters the glass of water, and how it reaches your eye.

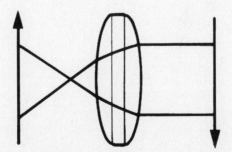

The Broken Pencil

While you have the water glass handy, find a pencil. Holding it vertically, dip the point of the pencil into the water.

Move either your head or the glass so that your eyes are directly in line with the surface of the water. Tip the pencil a little from side to side. Lift it up in the water just a bit. The illustration below shows what you'll see. Once again, the "convex" water has bent the light, and the pencil in it.

Many years ago a state had a law because of this sort of optical illusion. The law said that a person who saw a crime committed on the other side of a glass window could not be a witness. In those days the hand-crafted glass was convex, so windows would create this illusion.

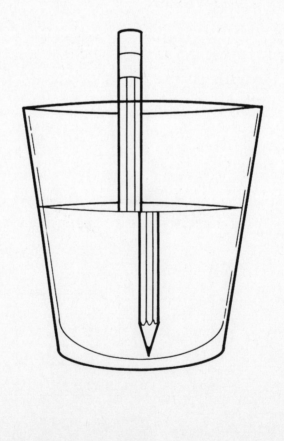

Two-Faced

Look at this illustration.
Now, turn the page upside down and look at the drawing again.
See how much can change with just a little movement?

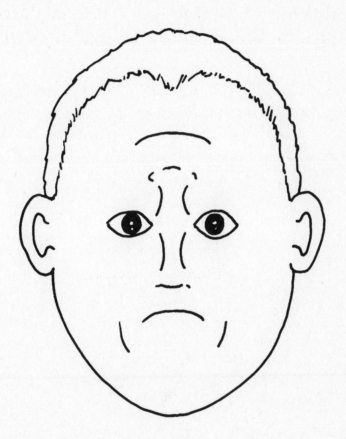

See-throughs

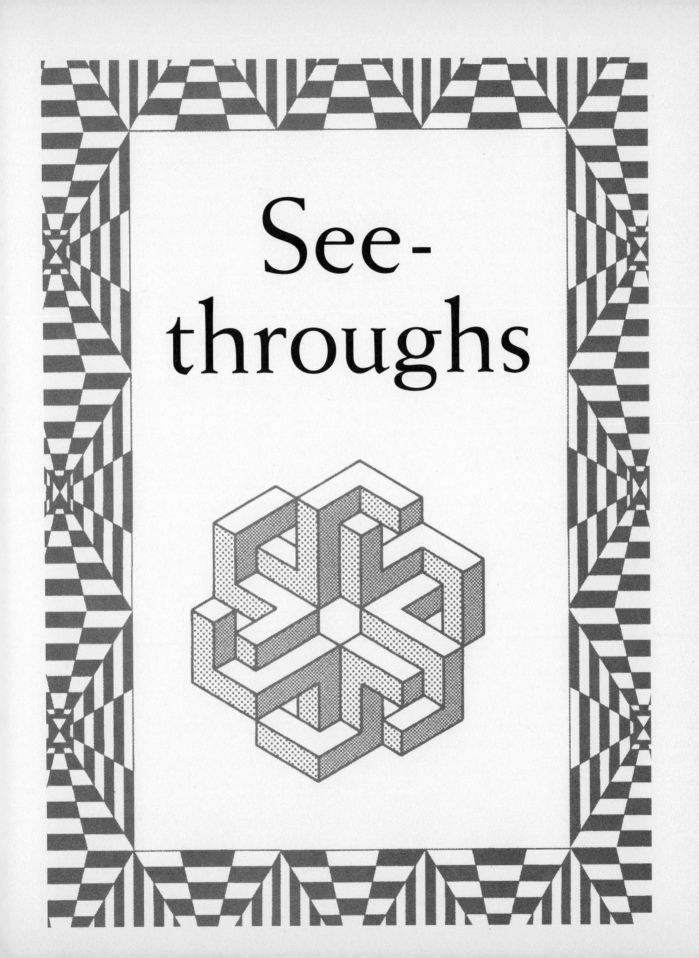

The Pinwheel

There is nothing new about a pinwheel, these toys have been around for hundreds of years. However, there is something about this toy which you may never have realized.

First, let's make a pinwheel. You'll need a piece of square notebook or typing paper. To make a rectangular piece of paper square, fold the bottom corner up as shown in the illustration below on the left. Cut away the shaded part of the paper. Unfold the paper and you have a perfect square.

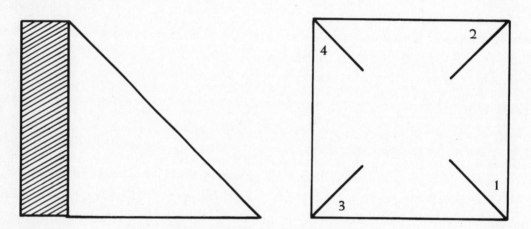

Make four cuts in this square piece of paper along the four dark lines as shown in the illustration above on the right. Each of these lines runs exactly halfway to the center.

The four lines in this same illustration each have a number. Begin with point 1 and bend (don't fold) it down to the middle of the paper. Push a pin through a point about ¼ inch from the tip of the point.

Now, bend point 2 over to the middle so that it is under point 1. Push the pin through it as well.

Do the same for points 3 and 4 and you have just about finished making your pinwheel.

It is a good idea to put a tiny dot of glue on the bottom of each point before adding the next point. This will keep the pinwheel's points together and make it spin better. If you don't have glue handy, a little piece of transparent tape works just as well. Be sure to glue or tape the last point to the main part of the pinwheel.

Mount your pinwheel on a long pencil with an eraser. Push the point of the pin into the eraser and the pencil becomes the handle of the pinwheel.

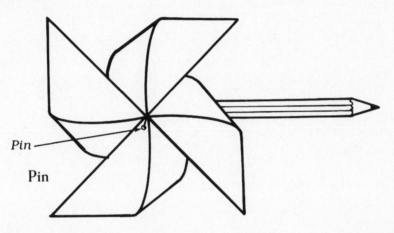

Pin

Pin

Hold the pinwheel in front of you so that the curved parts of the blades face forward. As you begin to walk, the wheel should spin, and the faster you walk, the faster it spins.

Now, look at something in front of the pinwheel as it spins. You can look right through the spinning pinwheel blades and see perfectly.

Examine your pinwheel, and you can easily see there is just as much paper as there is open space. Yet when the pinwheel spins rapidly you can see perfectly through its blades. The solid part almost vanishes.

Once again, afterimage is the culprit. Your eyes are focused on the object behind the pinwheel, so you actually only see the pinwheel in fleeting glimpses. Since your mind is also focused on the object instead of the pinwheel, it holds onto this image as long as possible. By the time it fades, your eyes see the object between the pinwheel parts again.

The Spinning Disc

Make a disc about 6 inches across out of the side of a cereal box or some other stiff material. If you don't have a compass, just draw around a dish or the lid from a small pan.

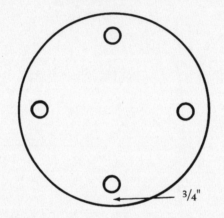

Now, cut four round holes in the disc as in the illustration above. Each of these holes should be about the size of a nickel. Make the outside edge of each little hole about ¾ inch from the outer edge of the disc.

Now, make two very small holes as shown in the illustration below. Each of these holes must be exactly ½ inch from the center of the disc.

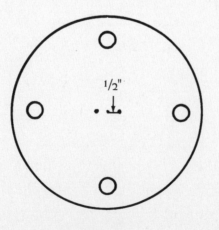

If you used a compass to draw your disc it is easy to find the center, but if not, trace around the disc on a sheet of paper. Cut out the paper circle which is the same size as your disc. Fold the circle in the middle

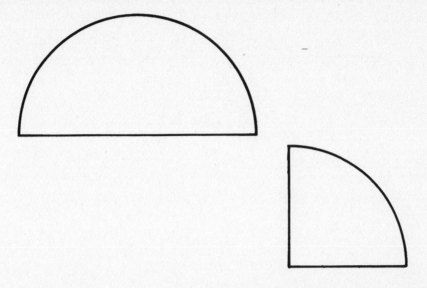

and crease the fold so that it looks like the illustration above on the left. Fold it double again so that it looks like the illustration on the right. Place the curve of this folded paper over the outside of your disc, and the point of the paper is the center of the disc.

Cut a piece of string about 4 feet long. Run both ends through the holes near the center of the disc, and tie the loose ends together so that your disc looks like the illustration below.

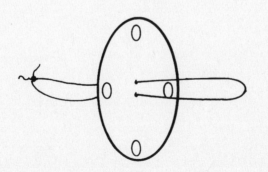

Slip two or three fingers into the loop at each end of the string. Spin the disc so that it makes a number of twists in the string. Be sure the disc remains at right angles to the string. The illustration below shows your disc ready to go.

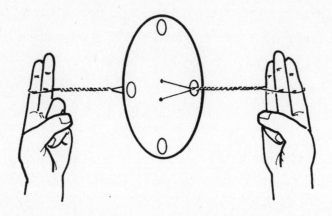

Pull your hands apart so that the disc spins as the string unwinds. Let its momentum start winding the string in the other direction. As this happens, allow your hands to begin to come together so that the string can wind up.

As the disc begins to slow, pull your hands apart and it will spin in the opposite direction. With practice, you can keep the disc spinning by moving your hands back and forth.

Now, look at the flat side of the spinning disc, and—surprise! Instead of seeing the four small holes flash past, there's a completely hollow ring. You can actually see through it as it spins.

If you have trouble keeping the disc at right angles, make one of thicker material, or, make two discs about 2 inches across, and glue one to each side of your disc around the center. Either way, all it takes is a bit of practice.

Narrow View

Moving optical illusions can take many forms. It's amazing to find out just what tricks our eyes can play on us.

Take a sheet of notebook or typing paper, and cut a narrow piece out of the middle of the paper so that it looks like the illustration below. The hole should be about 2 inches long and 1/4 inch wide.

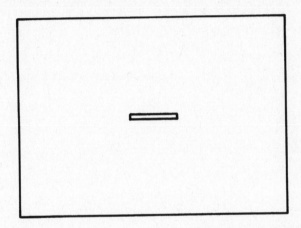

Lay the paper flat on any of the illustrations in this book. Be sure the narrow hole is over the middle of the picture. What do you see? Obviously, not much. Now begin moving the paper rapidly back and forth so that the opening slides up and down over the picture.

It takes only a few moves of the paper for you to realize that something strange is happening. You can actually see the entire picture, and the faster you move the paper, the clearer the picture becomes.

If you feel like experimenting, try this with another sheet of paper. This time make the narrow cut even narrower — less than 1/4 inch across. Keep the length 2 inches.

Can you still move the paper rapidly enough to see the picture? How small can you make the cut and still be able to see a picture under the sheet of paper?

See-through Grid

While you're looking through things, try a grid. This moving illusion has been around for many years. Your grandparents may have done it when they were children.

Start with a small piece of tracing paper. Tissue paper works well; even very thin typing paper works. Check it by placing it over this page to make sure you can still see the print through the paper.

To make the grid, rule off a square about 2 inches in each direction of your see-through paper. Don't cut out the square because you need to have a little margin on at least one side to hold on to.

Draw parallel lines up and down every 1/8 inch until you fill the square. Then draw another set of parallel lines across the square. These lines should also be 1/8 inch apart. Your grid should now look like this:

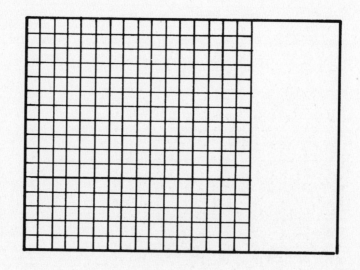

Now, draw parallel diagonal lines every 1/8 inch from right to left across the square. Finish up the grid with a final series of parallel diagonal lines from left to right. The final grid is shown below.

Place the finished grid over this page. When you try to read what the page says through the grid, it is almost impossible.

Take hold of the edge of the grid paper where you left some margin around the grid. Begin moving the grid rapidly back and forth over the print you want to read.

What happens to the lines on the grid? What happens to the print on the page beneath the grid?

Afterimage strikes again. Remember, there *is* space between the lines. Once you focus on the page under the grid your brain will try to help you see the page as clearly as possible. When the grid moves, your eyes will focus on the page and your brain ignores the lines that move back and forth. So, when your eyes see the grid, your brain still holds the afterimage, and as it fades, your eyes see the object again.

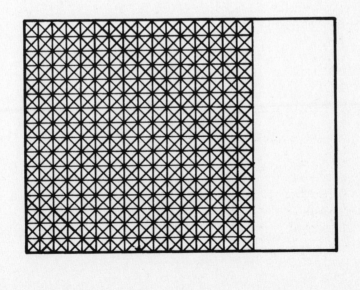

Seen Under Glass

Place a small, flat object on the table or on the countertop. A coin works fine: so does a paper clip or even a small piece of paper.

On top of this object, set a glass. Be sure that this is a clear glass that you can see through. Look through the glass from the top and the sides. Of course, you see the object beneath the glass.

Now, fill the glass with water. Get it as full as you can without spilling. Set it on top of the object. Look through the glass full of water. You'll see the object under the glass again. So, where is the illusion?

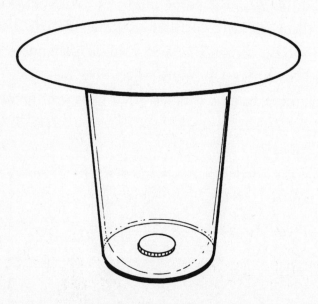

Place a saucer or a plastic lid from a butter tub on top of the glass, as shown above. Look through the side of the glass.

Remember that when light rays pass through water they are bent or turned at a different angle. When the saucer is on top of the glass the light rays which bend towards the top of the glass hit the saucer, shutting them in. The light rays from the coin can't be seen, so it seems to have vanished.

Strange Motion

Cut a circle 5 inches or so across from the side of a cereal carton. Any stiff material works fine but cereal cartons are usually pretty easy to find.

Make the cut shown below.

1/2"

Be careful when you poke the point of your scissors through the cardboard. You want a hole in the cardboard, not your finger.

The little cut should be 1 inch long, 1/8 inch wide, and about 1/2 inch from the outside of the cardboard disc.

Next, find the exact center of the disc and make a small hole there. If you forgot how to find the circle's center, look back at page 173. It works every time.

Push a pencil through the center so that it looks like the illustration below.

Hold the pencil between your hands. Keep both hands flat and press them together firmly against the pencil.

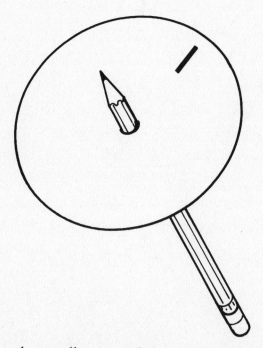

Rub your hands rapidly up and down so that the pencil spins back and forth between your hands. When the pencil spins, the disc will spin as well.

If the disc slips on the pencil, use several pieces of tape to fasten it to the main part of the pencil.

Start a record turntable without a record on it. Place a piece of paper or cardboard on one side of the turntable, as shown here.

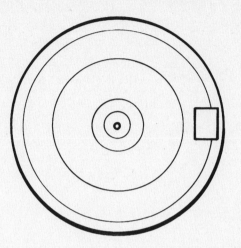

As the turntable turns, spin the disc between your hands. Look directly at the turntable through the narrow little slit in the disc. What's happening to the paper on the turntable? Is it actually jumping back and forth? It can't be.

Try spinning your disc faster or slower to see how this affects the way the paper on the turntable seems to act.

Do you have fluorescent lights around you? These are the ones which have the long tubes. Lots of classrooms have them.

Look at a fluorescent light through your spinning disc. If you get the speed just right, you can get the light to blink on and off like a flashing strobe light you would see at a concert or disco.

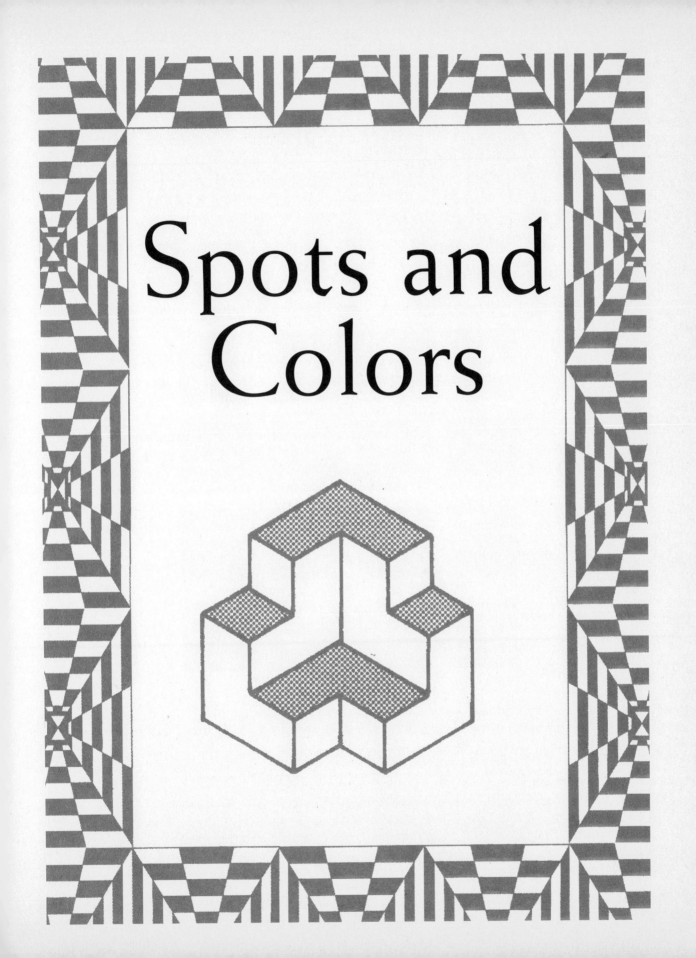

Spots and Colors

The Case
of the Moving Spots

Look at this illustration. Everywhere white lines meet, you should see something interesting.

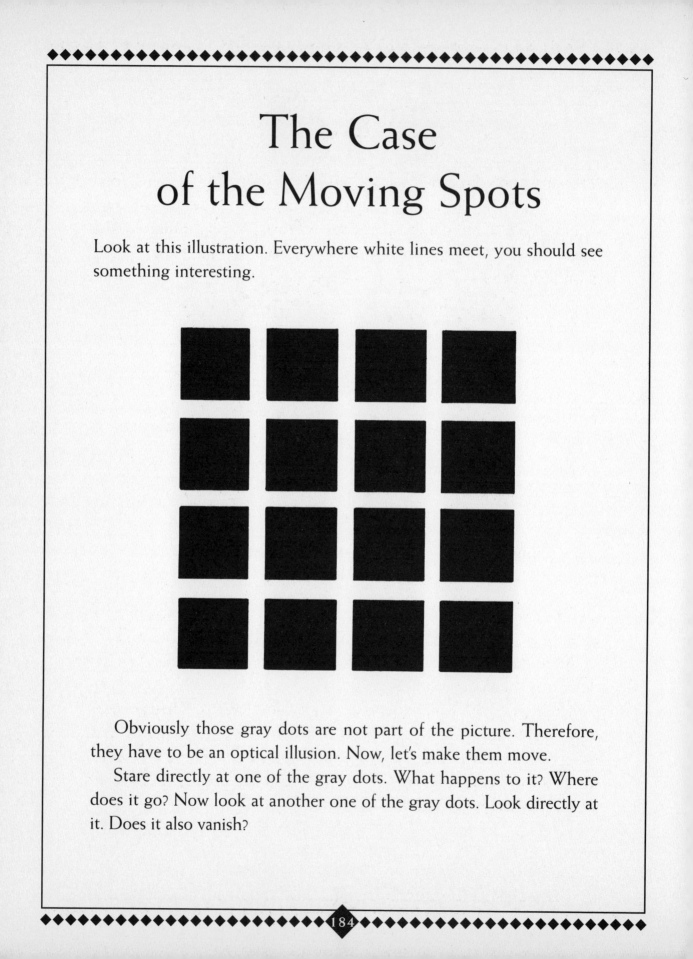

Obviously those gray dots are not part of the picture. Therefore, they have to be an optical illusion. Now, let's make them move.

Stare directly at one of the gray dots. What happens to it? Where does it go? Now look at another one of the gray dots. Look directly at it. Does it also vanish?

Floaters

Make a tiny hole in a piece of paper or a white file card. This is called a pin-hole. If the hole you make is a little larger than a pinhole, that is just fine.

Now hold the tiny hole up to your eye. Stare at a light through the hole. *Don't stare at the sun.* A shaded lamp should be bright enough. The illustration below shows how to manage this.

Close the eye not looking through the pinhole, and focus on the hole itself; you will begin to see slow-moving little circles or rings.

After a minute check your other eye. The same sorts of hollow little circles should appear.

These slowly moving little fellows are called floaters. They actually move inside your eyeball. These tiny floaters are normal and do not mean anything is wrong with your eyes. From time to time little cells inside the eye come free and float in the liquid which fills your eyeball. That's why they're called floaters.

Most people have another kind of floater inside their eyes. The way to check for these is to look down at the floor for a few seconds; then quickly raise your head and look at a light-colored wall. You may see one or more tiny little dark-colored objects which seem to be between you and the wall.

Don't worry if you can't see any floaters. Older people are more likely to have them than children, and some young people don't seem to have them at all. Remember, though, when you glance up and suddenly see a few little moving spots out in space, the funny little dark spots really are inside your eye.

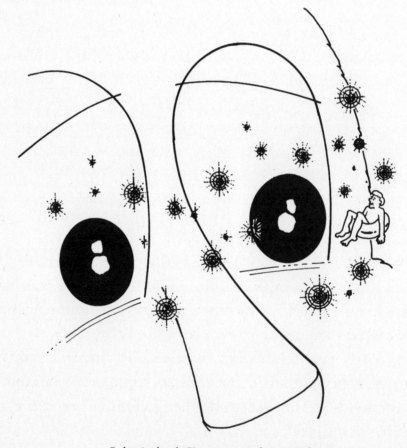

I don't think I'm supposed to see that!

Colorful Illusion

Begin by making a bright orange triangle on a white piece of paper. A triangle about 1 inch high is a good size.

Now, make a card with a pinhole and, holding the orange triangle out in front of you, peer through the hole in the card as shown here.

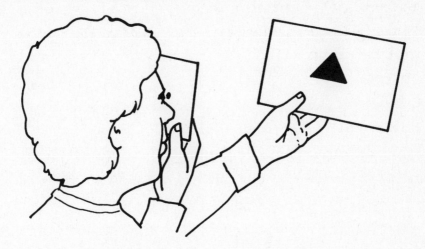

What happens to the brightness of the orange triangle? Did the color fade or is it just an illusion?

Try this one. On a white piece of paper make a solid red square, about 1 inch across. Stare directly at it for about thirty seconds; then look away and focus on a white piece of paper or a white wall. Within a few seconds a square will appear. But it won't be red!

Now, color a green circle on a piece of white paper. It's okay to use the paper with the red square, but fold the red square over out of sight. Stare at it intently for half a minute; then look at a sheet of clean white paper. What color is it?

Do the same thing with the orange triangle you made before. Stare at it; see what color the orange triangle becomes when you look away.

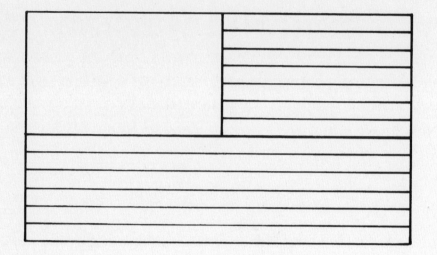

The illustration above should be familiar to you. Make the outline of the flag about 6¹/₂ inches high x 10 inches. The smaller rectangle at the upper left should be about 5 inches wide and 3¹/₂ inches high. Each of the 13 bands should be exactly ¹/₂ inch wide.

Color the small rectangle orange; then color the top band green and the second band black, alternating the bands, green and black, all the way to the bottom. You will end up with the bottom band colored green. There should be seven green bands and six black bands. Make your colors good and dark. Somehow it doesn't look right, does it?

Now, stare intently at the finished picture for about thirty seconds; then look away at a sheet of white paper or a white wall. It should look a little more familiar now. If you want, add some black dots to the orange field. Alternate five rows of six dots with four rows of five dots. If you begin and end with a row of six dots, you've done it perfectly.

This is a project you will probably want to put up on your wall or bulletin board. Place a sheet of white paper beside it so that others can see the illusion move from the original to the plain white page.

Spinning Colors

About 150 years ago some German scientists discovered a way to make black and white drawings look colorized. They discovered a disc that is still a great illusion today.

The first disc you will make is shown here.

Make this disc as large as you wish, but 3½ inches across is a good size. Use any stiff white material (a 4 x 5-inch file card is perfect).

If you don't have stiff white cardboard, make your circle on white paper, color it, and cut it out. Glue or tape it to any stiff material (like a cereal box).

A soft-tipped marker is excellent for coloring, but a black crayon will also do the job.

Color half the disc solid black; then put in the two sets of curved black lines. A compass or the edge of a round object can help with these curved lines.

Try to space the curves evenly. Draw them in pencil first; then go over the pencil lines with marker or crayon. If the spaces between the lines are not exactly the same the project will still work, so don't panic. Once the disc is colored it is time to see whether those German scientists knew what they were talking about.

First we need to spin the disc. There are three ways to do this.

One is to stick a straight pin through the center of the disc, making sure the head of the pin is at the front (so the disc won't spin off). Hold the pointed end of the pin tightly, and use your other hand to do the spinning.

A second way to spin is to push the point of a pencil through the disc's center. Hold the pencil between your palms and rub your hands back and forth. This spins the disc quickly in one direction, then back in the other. A straight-sided pencil works better than a round one. A couple of pieces of tape to attach the back of the disc to the sides of the pencil should also help.

The third way is to use the string spinner. If you forgot how to make one of these, look back at page 172. If you have any trouble keeping the spinner upright, just use a couple of pieces of tape on the back of the spinner so that the tape sticks to the strings as they go through the spinner. The illustration below shows how to do this.

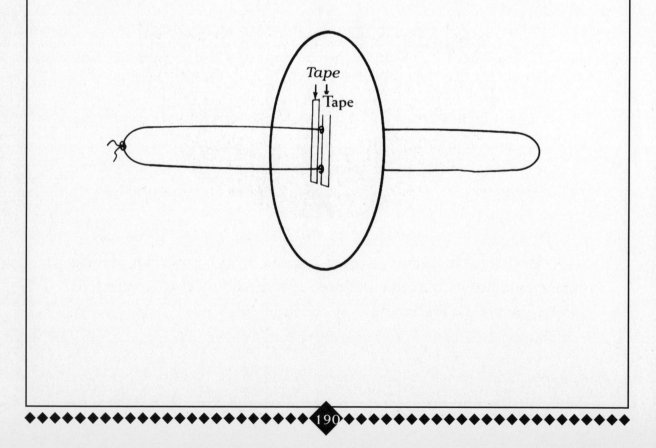

Give your disc a good spin. Watch what happens to the black and white design. If you don't see the colors at first, don't give up. Spin it some more, and take a good look.

You should see brown and blue appear. When the disc turns one way, the brown is towards the outside of the disc. When it spins the other way, blue is outside. Check it for yourself.

The illustration below shows another black and white disc which will turn to different colors when it spins. Make it the same way you made the previous disc.

When this disc spins, you should be able to spot the colors of blue, green, and brown. Just like the first disc, the colors change positions when you reverse the direction of the spin.

Color Wheel

You have probably seen a color wheel in the art room at school. It shows colors in special order. It's also an interesting spinning optical illusion.

Make a disc 3½ inches across. This time make it exact, because 3½ inches across is lots easier to divide into 21 equal parts. That's right, 21.

Use a ruler to measure along the outside of the disc and place a dot every ½ inch. If all goes well you will finish with 21 equal spaces. If the last space is a tiny bit larger or smaller than the others, it won't ruin the project.

The illustration on the facing page shows the disc with all those lines in place. It also tells what color to use in coloring each section of the disc.

Color each section of the disc according to this key: W=white, R=red, O=orange, Y=yellow, G=green, B=blue, and V=violet (purple). Colored pencils are easier to use than crayons, but crayons will do the job if you have a steady hand.

Once the disc is colored, give it a spin. As it moves faster and faster, you will see it change color. If you can get the disk to spin fast enough you will see only a white disc. More likely you will see a very light tan or even a light gray.

When the disc stops, there are all those colors, still in place. The light color was just another optical illusion.

More Visual Trickery

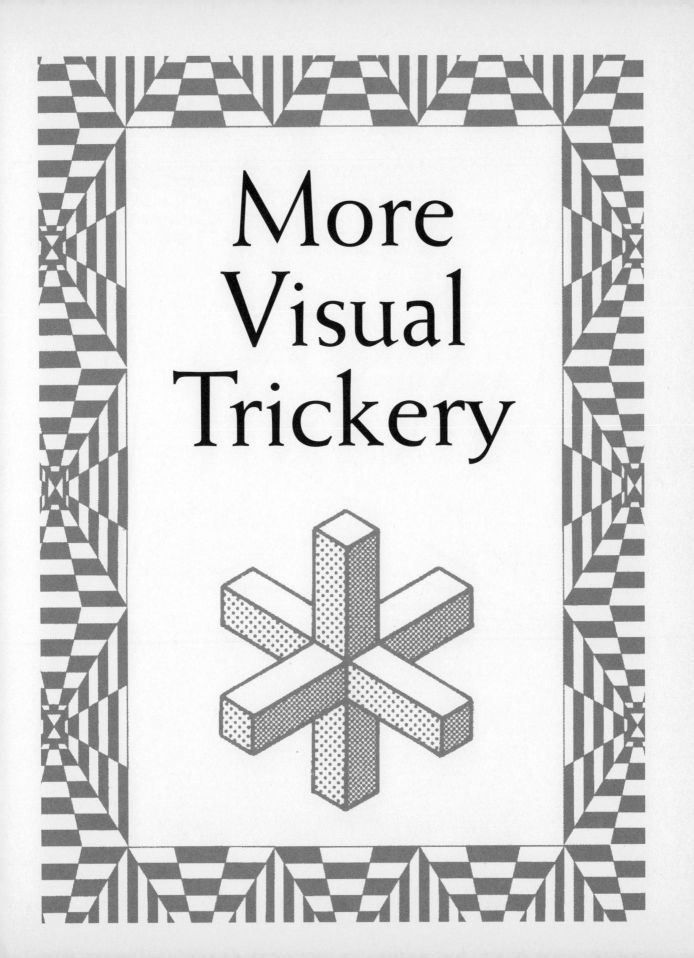

How many triangles can you find in this design?

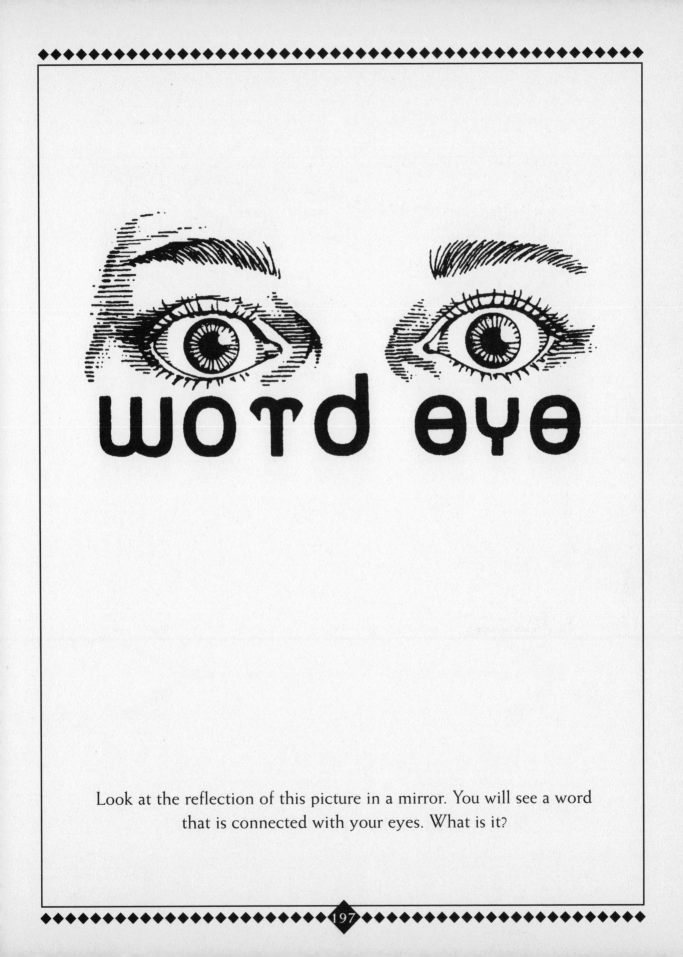

Look at the reflection of this picture in a mirror. You will see a word that is connected with your eyes. What is it?

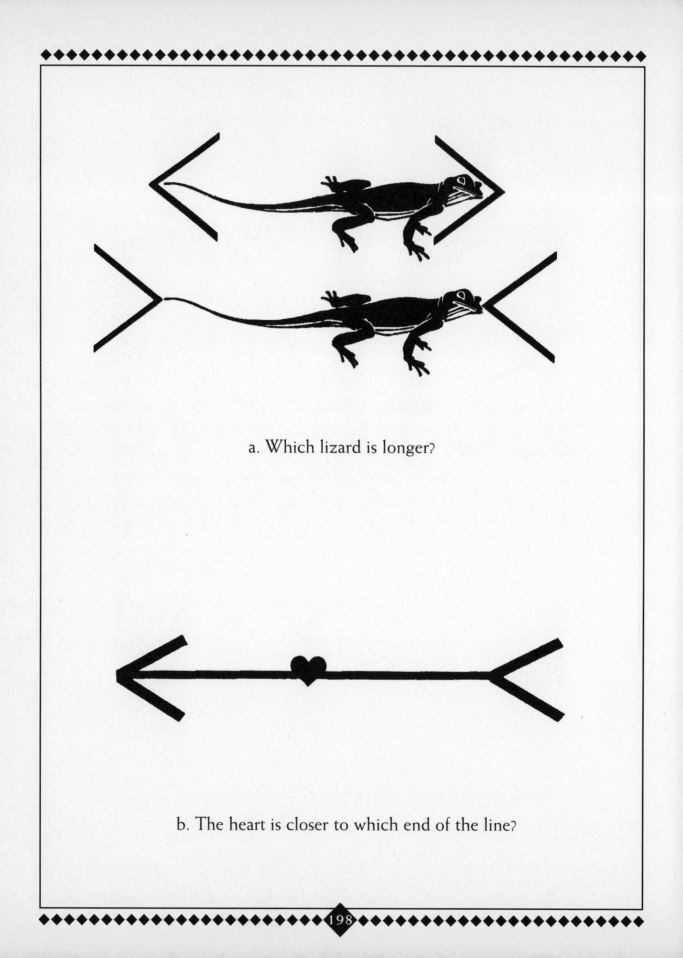

a. Which lizard is longer?

b. The heart is closer to which end of the line?

Is the middle square bulging out?

How about this square? Is it narrower on top?

What is unusual about this picture?

This student was very bright. Years later he became a professor. What do you think he looks like now?

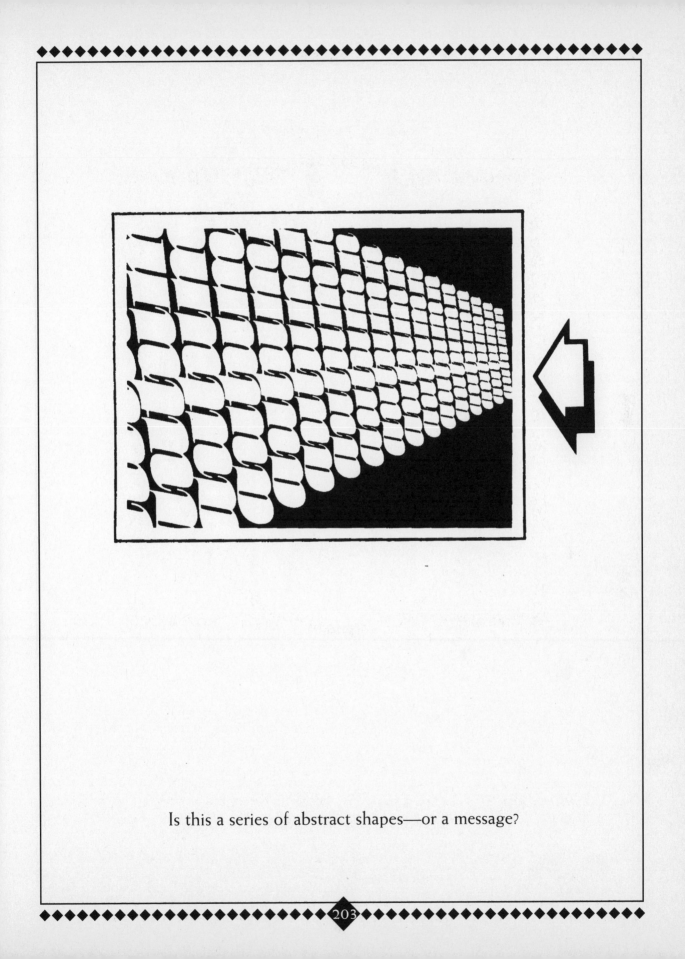

Is this a series of abstract shapes—or a message?

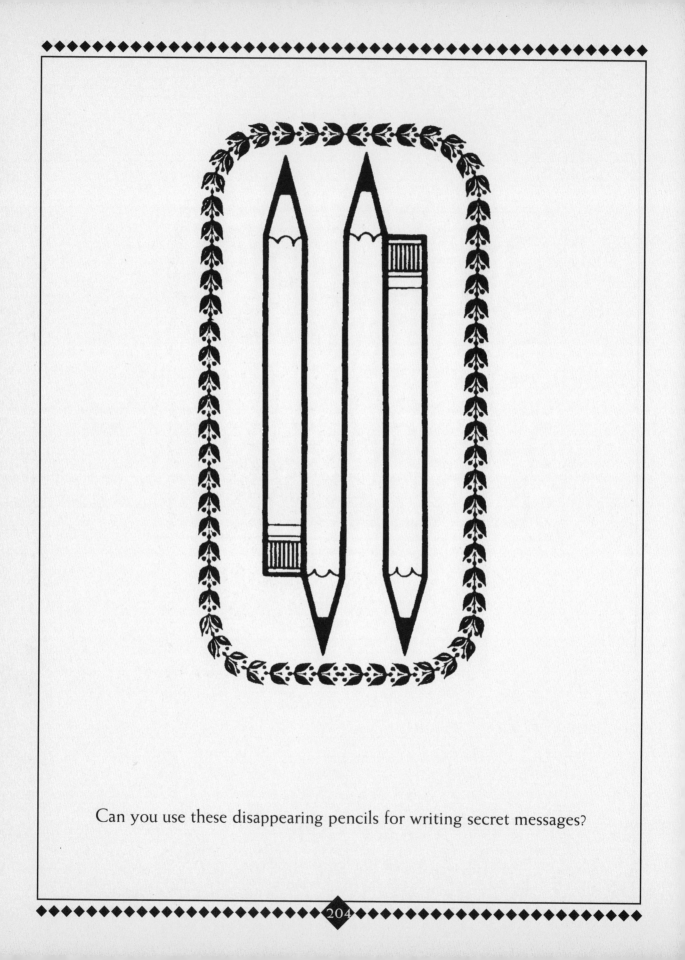

Can you use these disappearing pencils for writing secret messages?

This girl is enjoying the Magic Show, but where is the magician?

Which of these flowers has the larger center?

What's wrong with this picture?

Can you find this baby's mother?

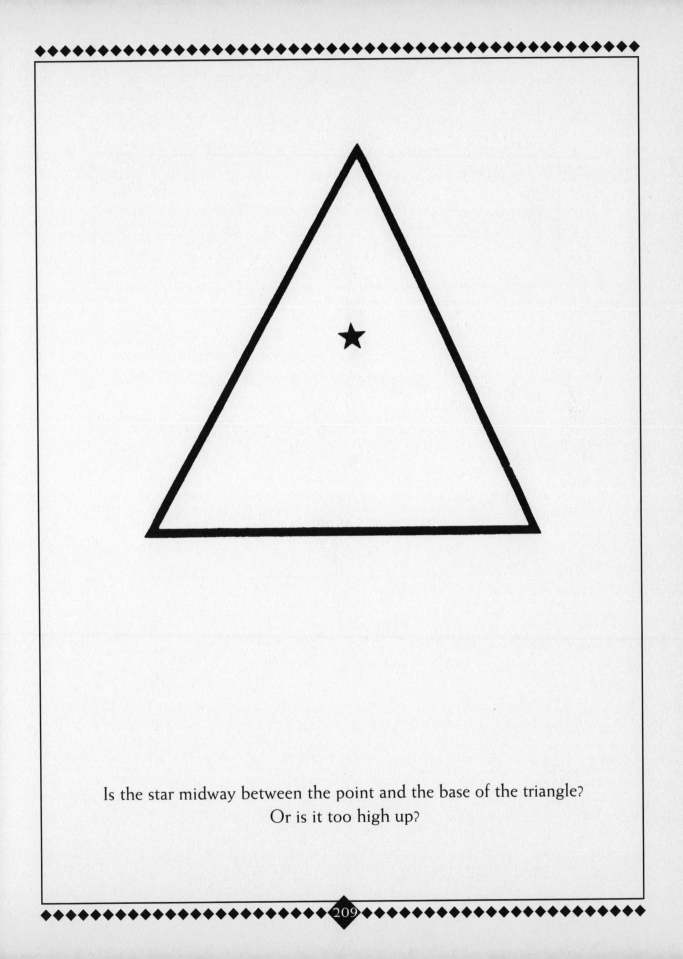

Is the star midway between the point and the base of the triangle?
Or is it too high up?

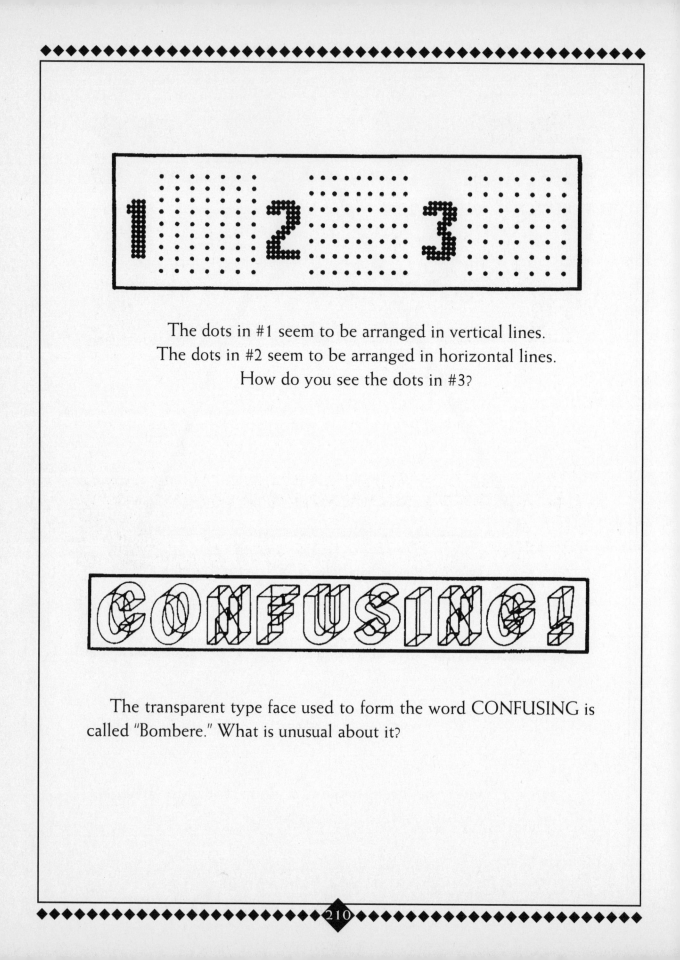

The dots in #1 seem to be arranged in vertical lines.
The dots in #2 seem to be arranged in horizontal lines.
How do you see the dots in #3?

The transparent type face used to form the word CONFUSING is
called "Bombere." What is unusual about it?

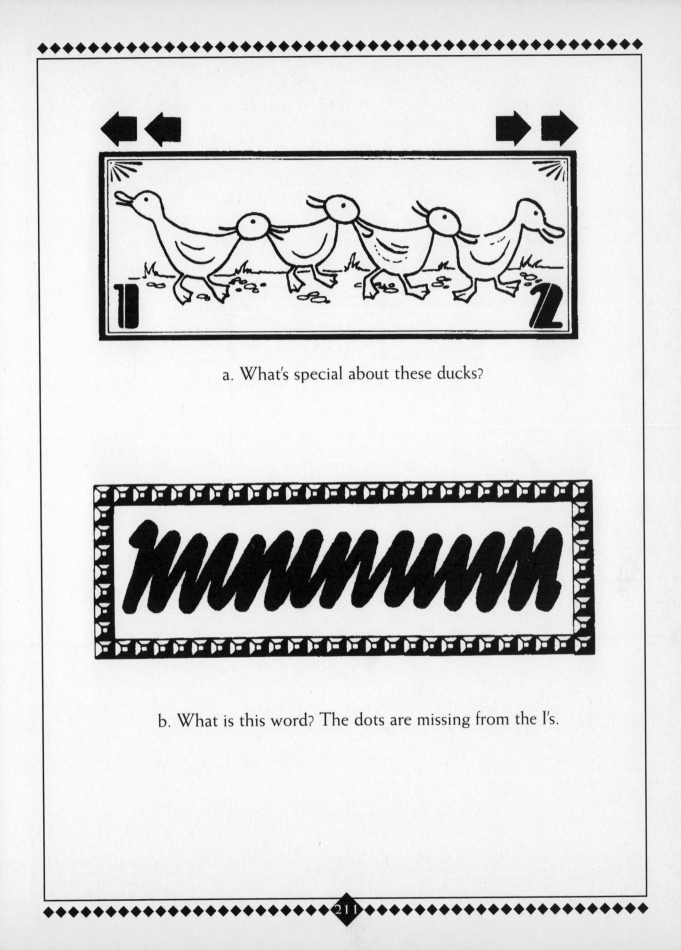

a. What's special about these ducks?

b. What is this word? The dots are missing from the I's.

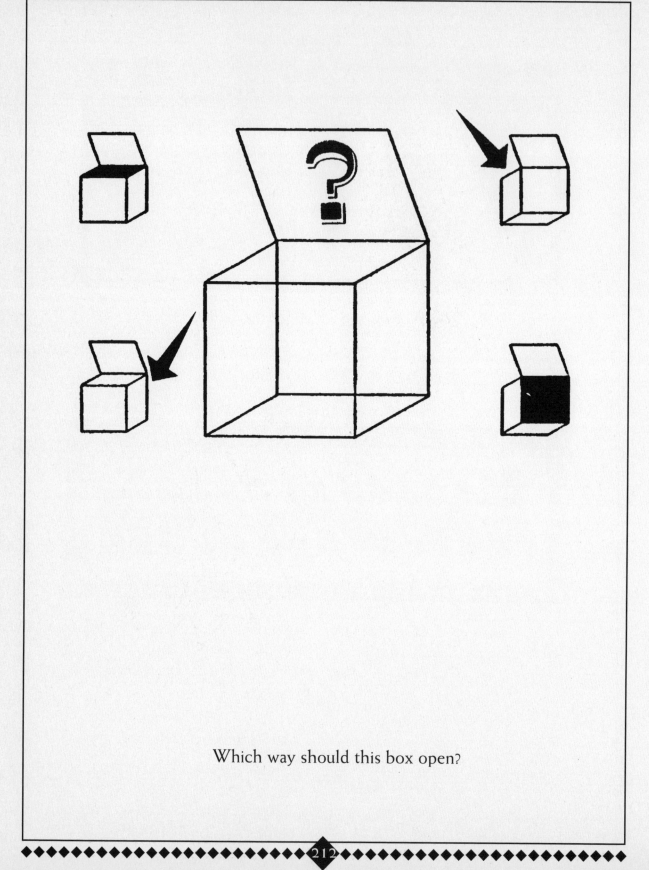

Which way should this box open?

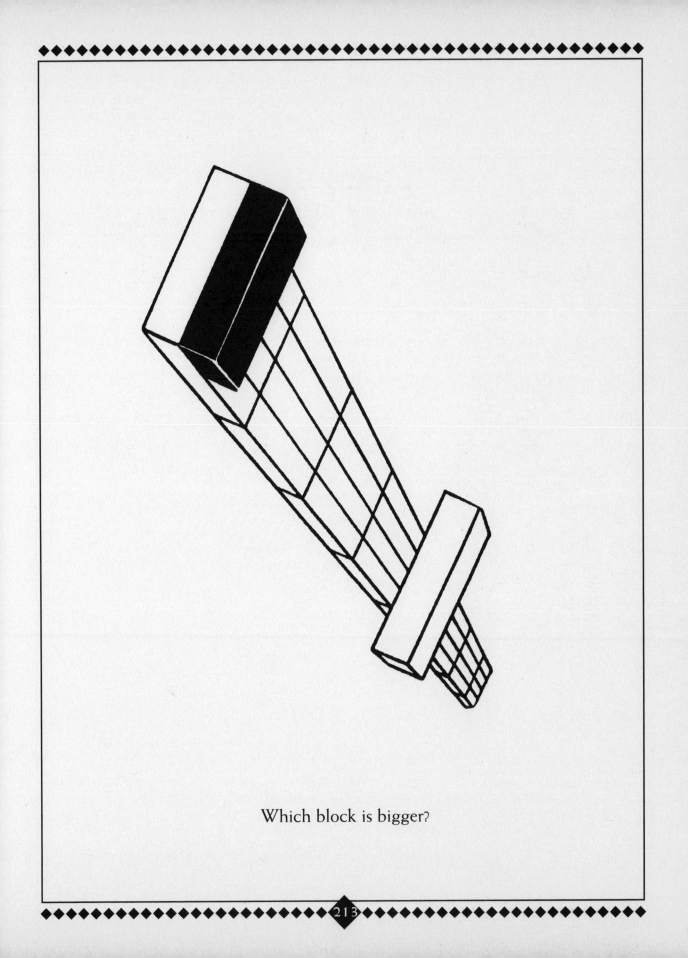

Which block is bigger?

Is the white circle perfect, or is it crimped at the points of the triangle?

This picture conceals the faces of two men. Can you find them?

Do you think the sides of the cloister arches are disjointed?
Or do they join up?

We read this sign as THE CAT, but the middle letters of each word
are identical. Yet we see them as H in THE and A in CAT.
Why is this?

What is the matter with the hoop that Geoffrey is holding?

What is this picture?

Is the square sagging at the right?

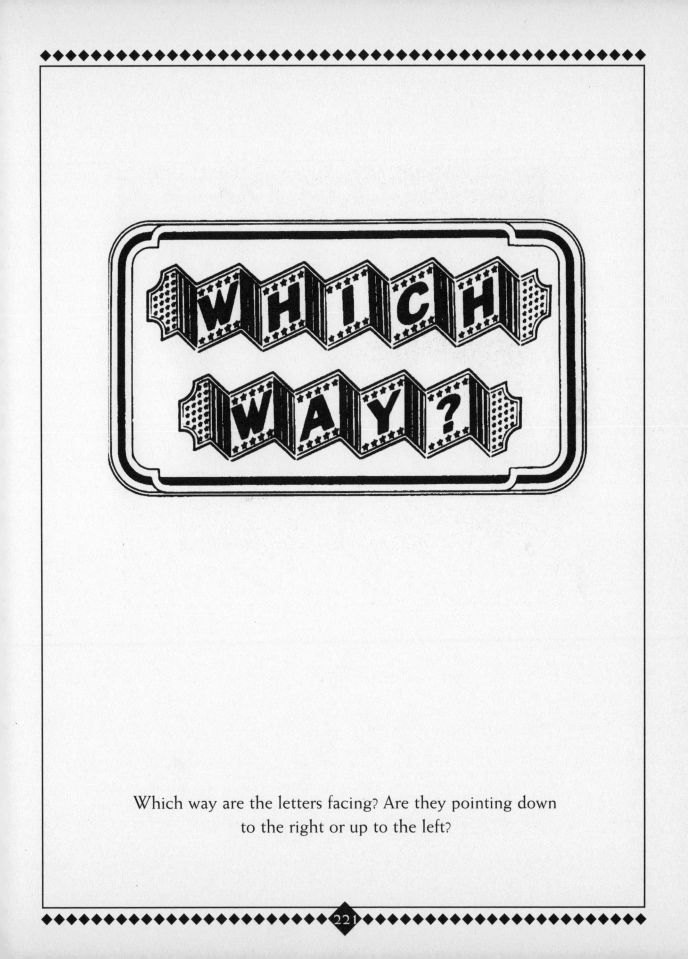

Which way are the letters facing? Are they pointing down
to the right or up to the left?

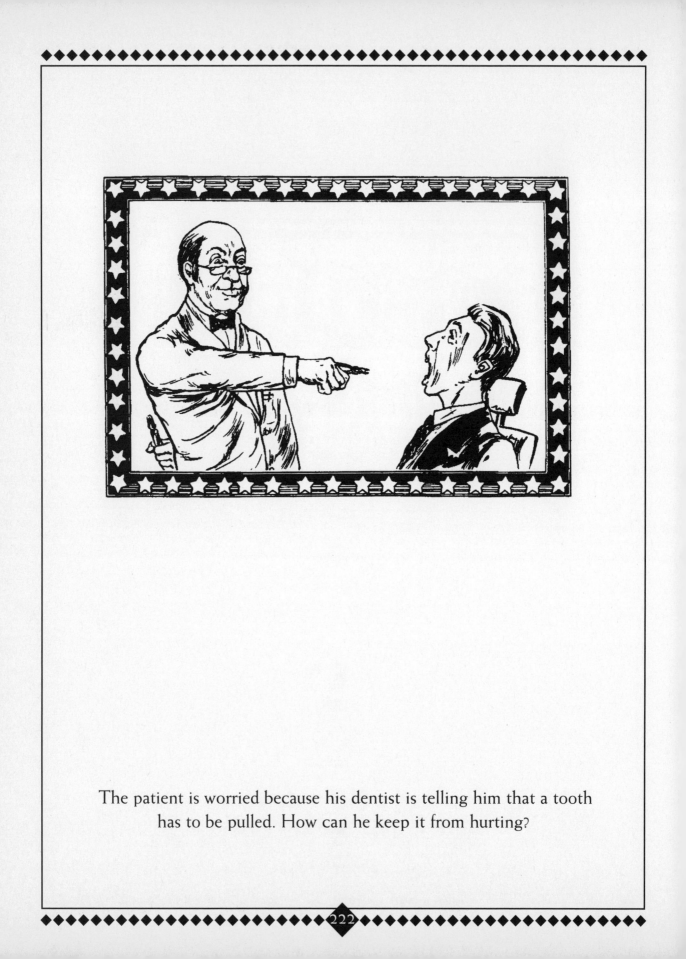

The patient is worried because his dentist is telling him that a tooth
has to be pulled. How can he keep it from hurting?

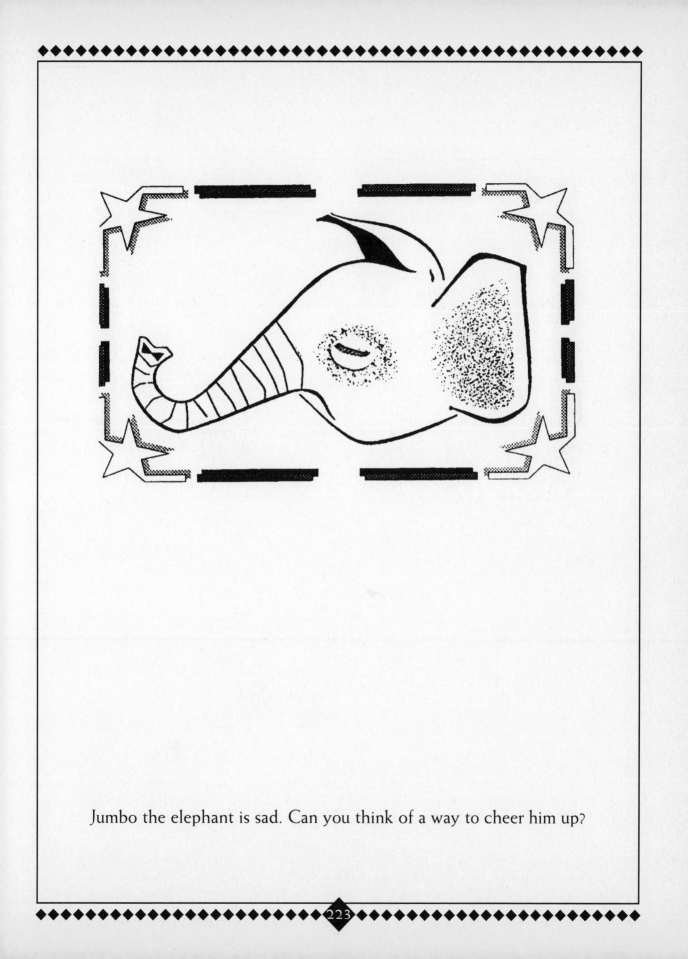

Jumbo the elephant is sad. Can you think of a way to cheer him up?

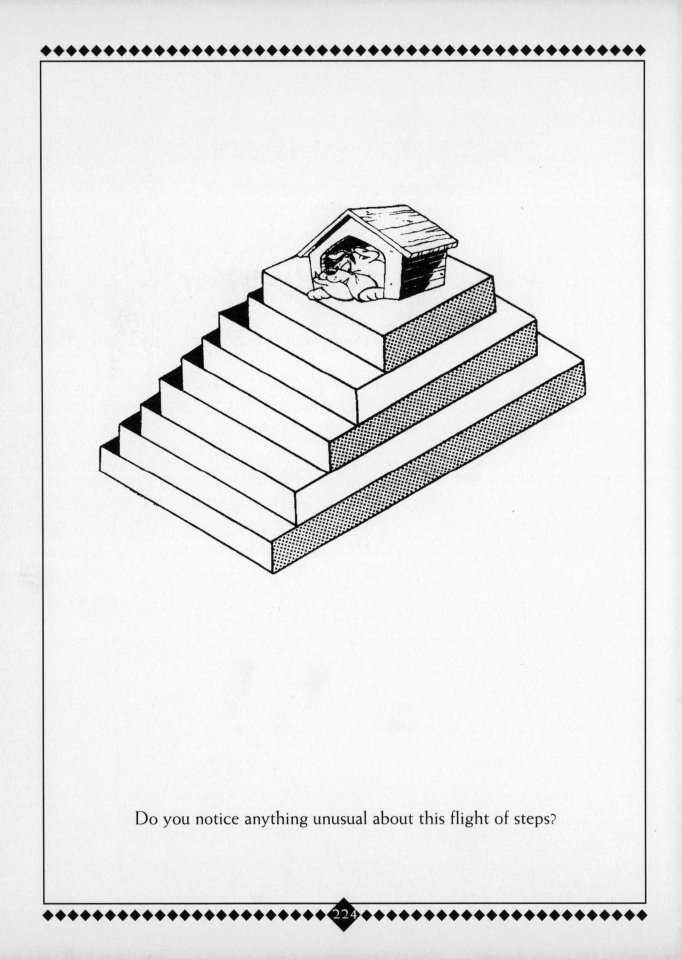

Do you notice anything unusual about this flight of steps?

This fellow helps Santa Claus. But where is Santa hiding?

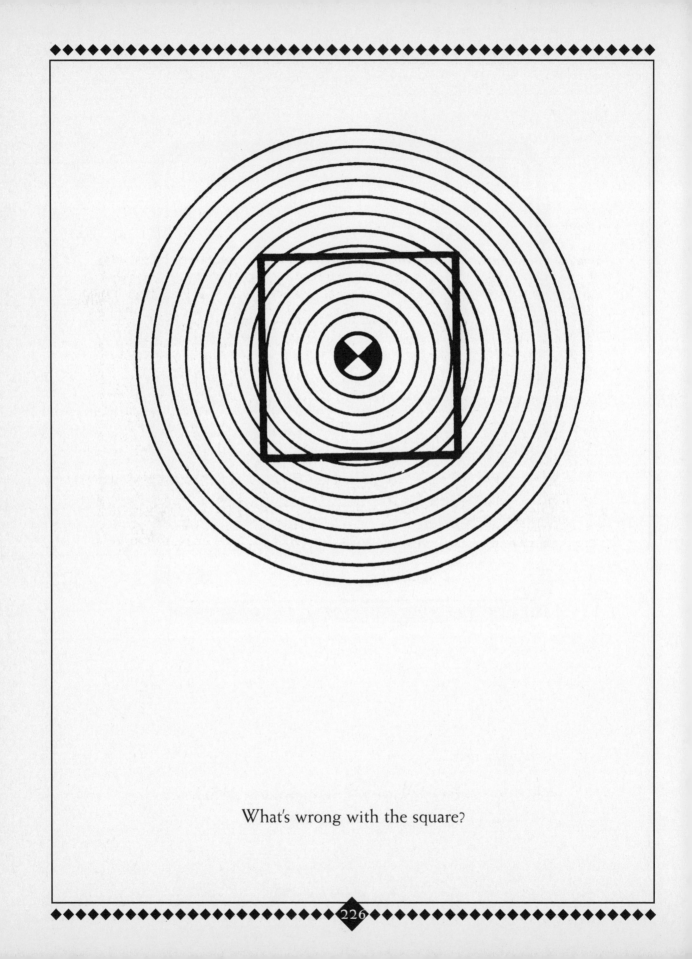

What's wrong with the square?

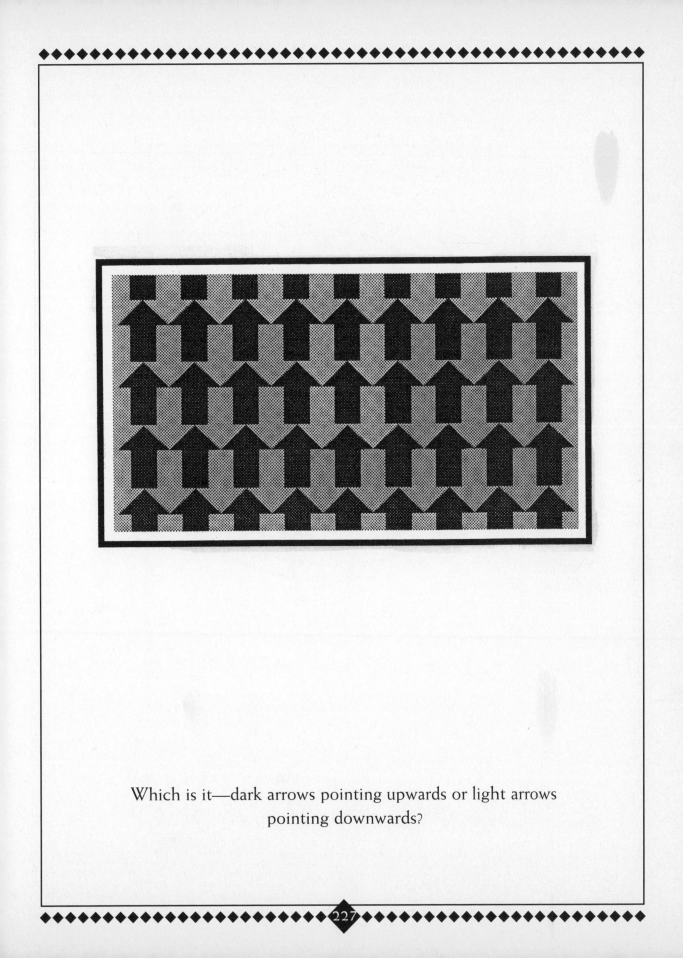

Which is it—dark arrows pointing upwards or light arrows
pointing downwards?

This soldier is looking for his horse. Any idea where it is?

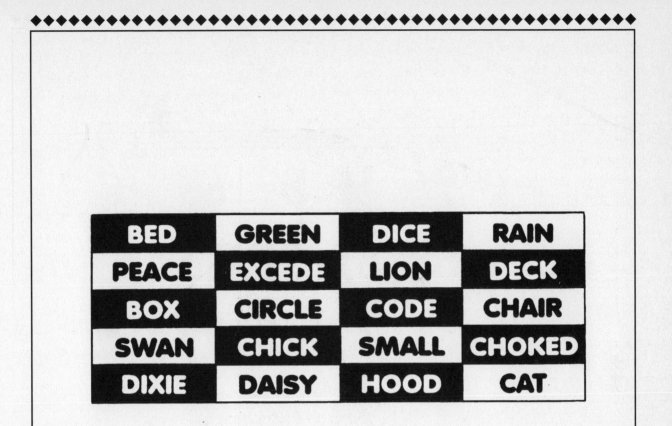

BED	GREEN	DICE	RAIN
PEACE	EXCEDE	LION	DECK
BOX	CIRCLE	CODE	CHAIR
SWAN	CHICK	SMALL	CHOKED
DIXIE	DAISY	HOOD	CAT

Using a mirror, turn this page upside down and look at the reflection of the letters. It's odd that all the words in the black panels can be read easily—but not those in the white panels. How and why do you think this happens?

What is special about this diagram?

Are these balls the same size?

Meet Barnacle Bill, the old sailor. What did he look like when
he was young?

Rotate the page in a circular motion. What happens?

Which set of faces is larger?

Is this a block with a piece cut out, or a block with a piece stuck on?

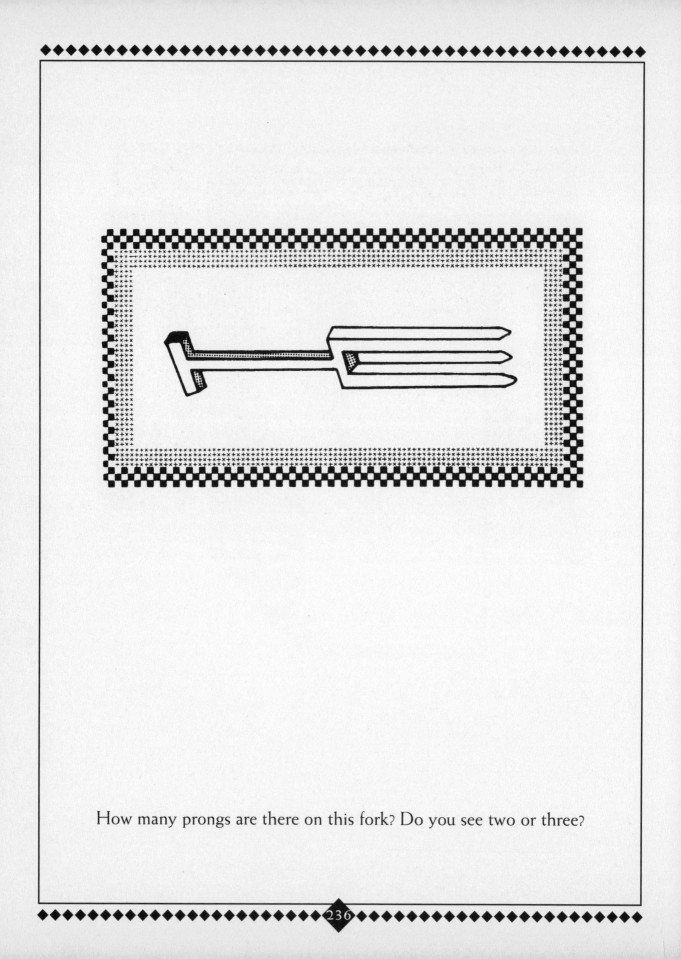

How many prongs are there on this fork? Do you see two or three?

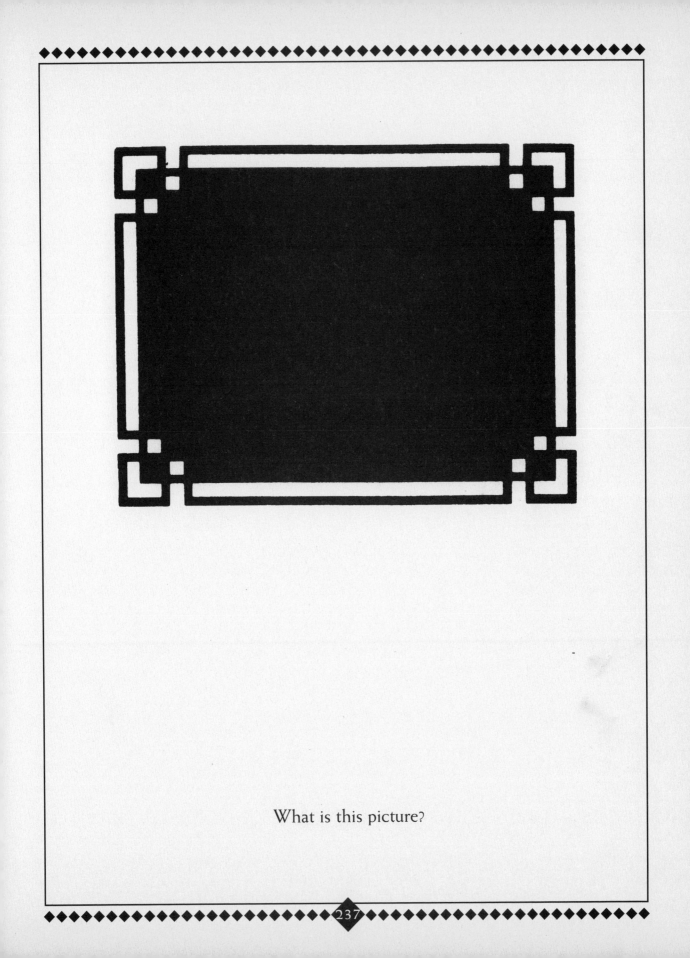

What is this picture?

Optical Tricks

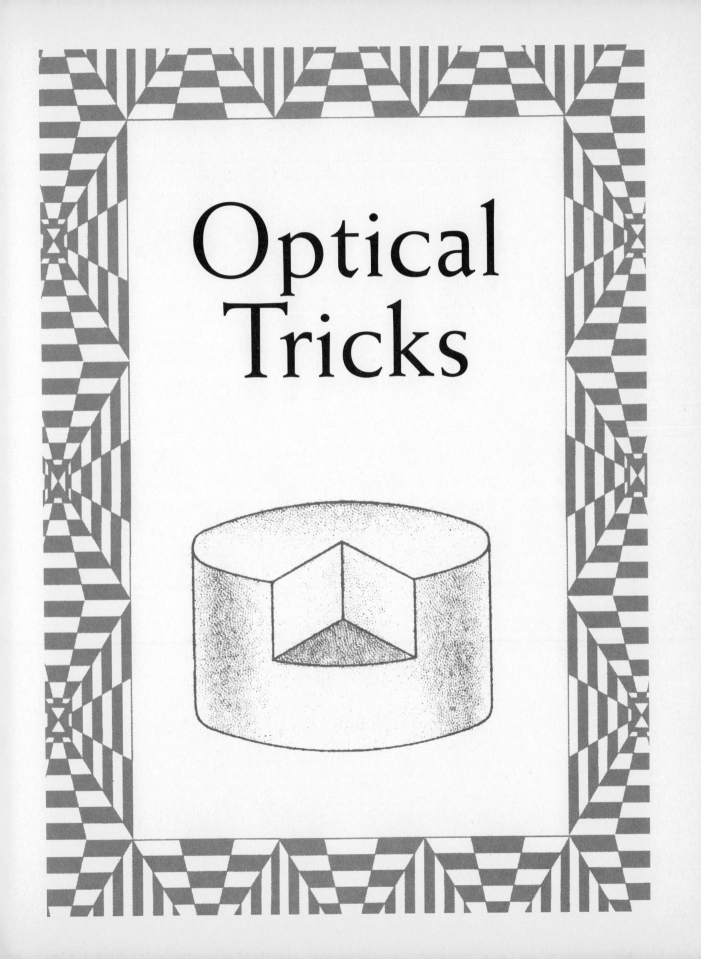

Which of these two boys has the wider mouth, A or B?

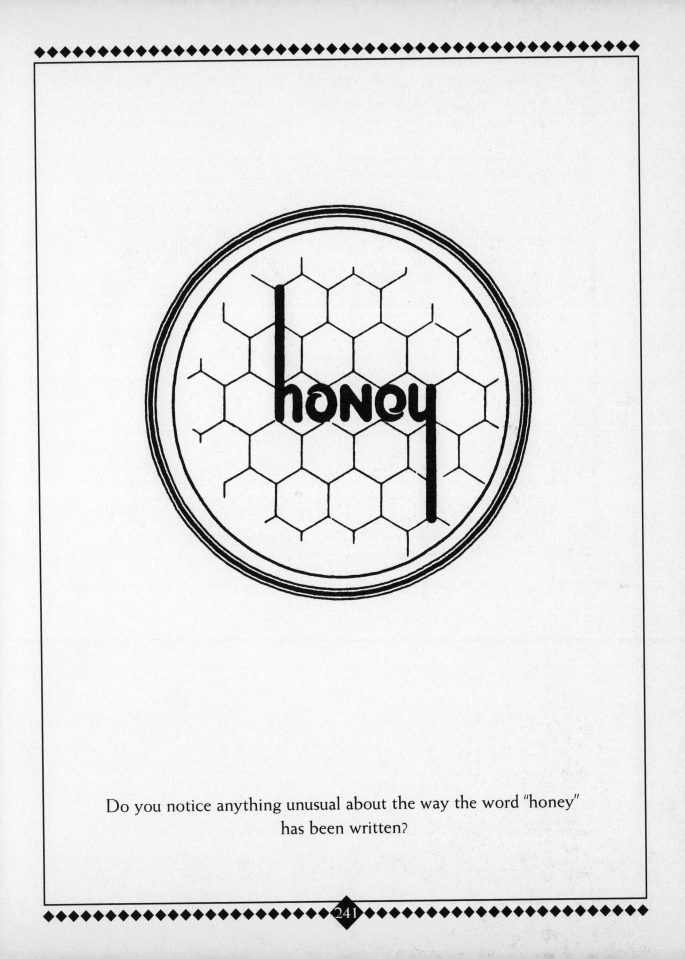

Do you notice anything unusual about the way the word "honey"
has been written?

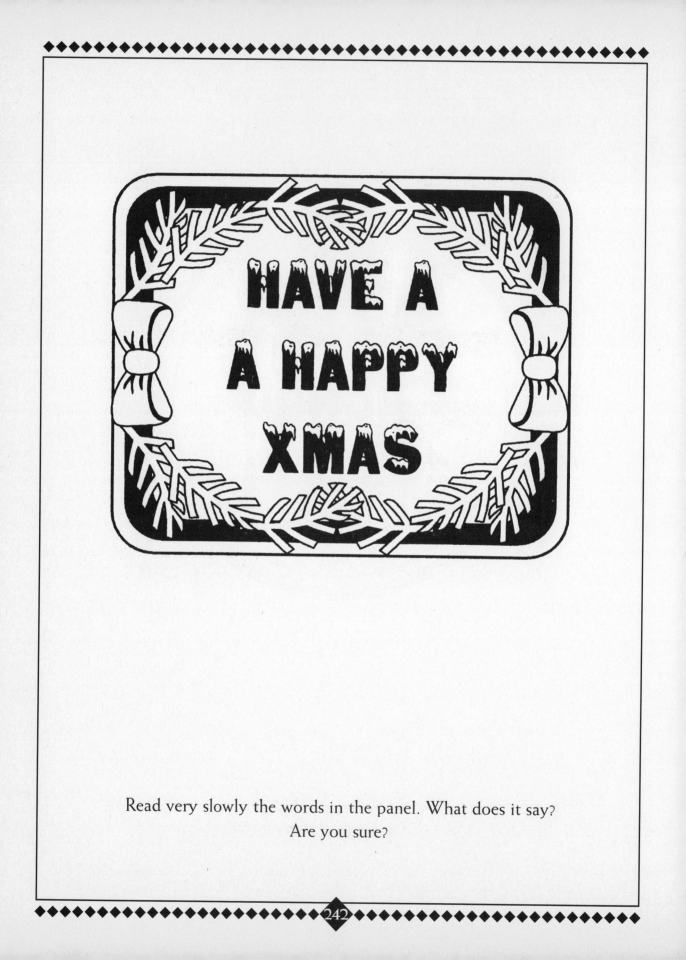

HAVE A A HAPPY XMAS

Read very slowly the words in the panel. What does it say?
Are you sure?

What do you see—four arrows pointing to the center or a standard cross with a diagonal cross behind it?

Which looks bigger, the brim or the height of Abraham Lincoln's
top hat?

Rotate very slowly this page with the hypnotic square.
What do you see?

Is this a black circle with two leg shapes or is it something else?

Stare at this picture without blinking for about 30 seconds. Then look at a sheet of white paper. Who do you see?

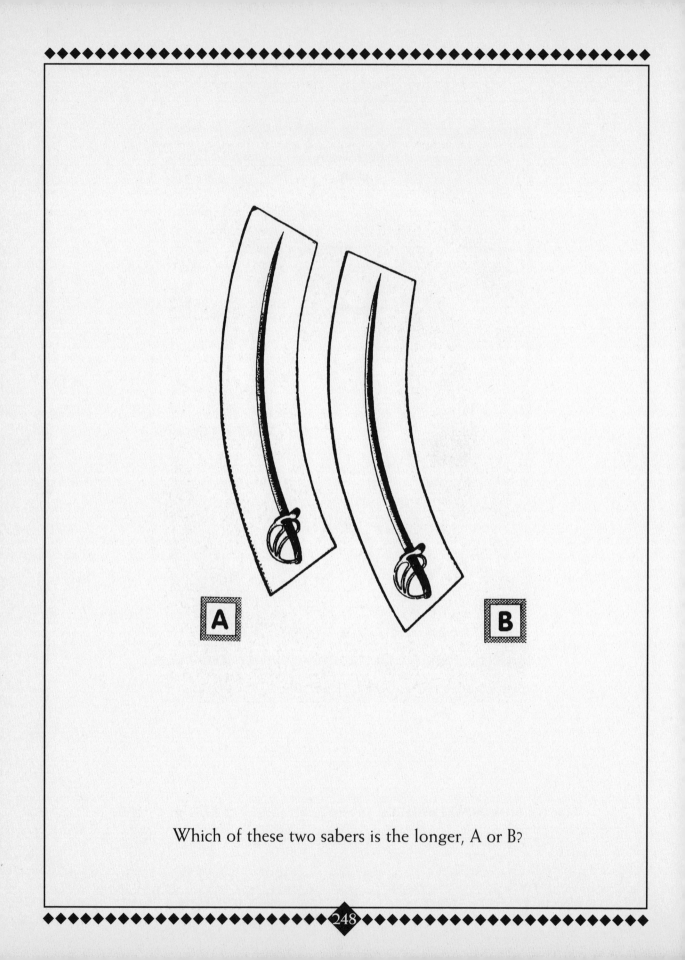

Which of these two sabers is the longer, A or B?

The sailor is looking through the telescope to find his girlfriend.
Can you find her?

This girl has a strange pet animal. Can you discover what it is?

What creature do you see here? Is it a hawk or a goose?

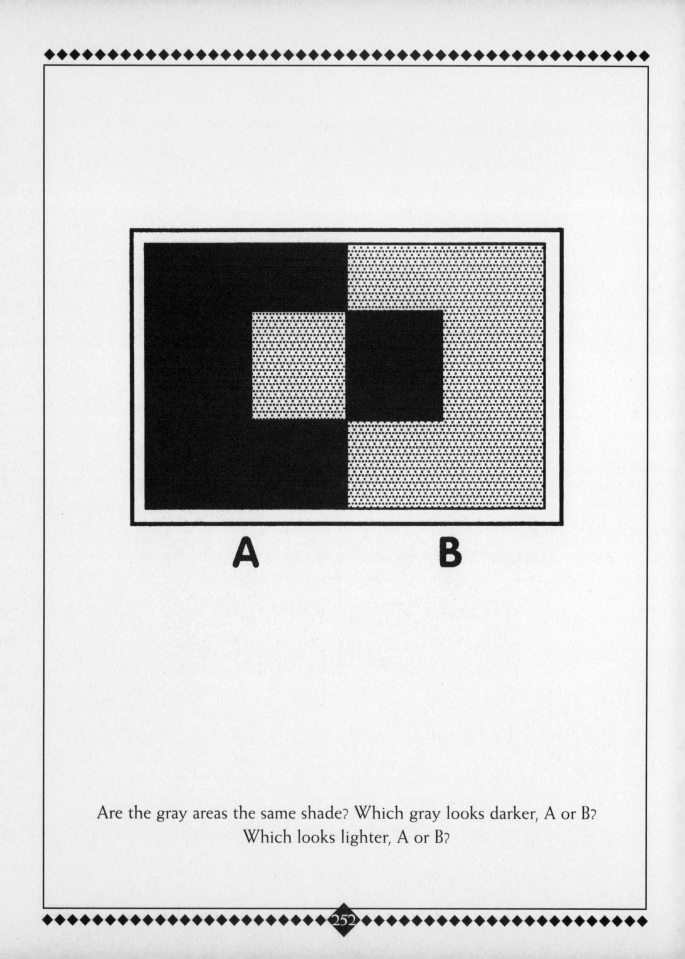

Are the gray areas the same shade? Which gray looks darker, A or B?
Which looks lighter, A or B?

Can you see where Napoleon is hiding?

Stare at the center of this illustration and then very slowly bring the page towards your face. What happens next?

Is this a perfect circle?

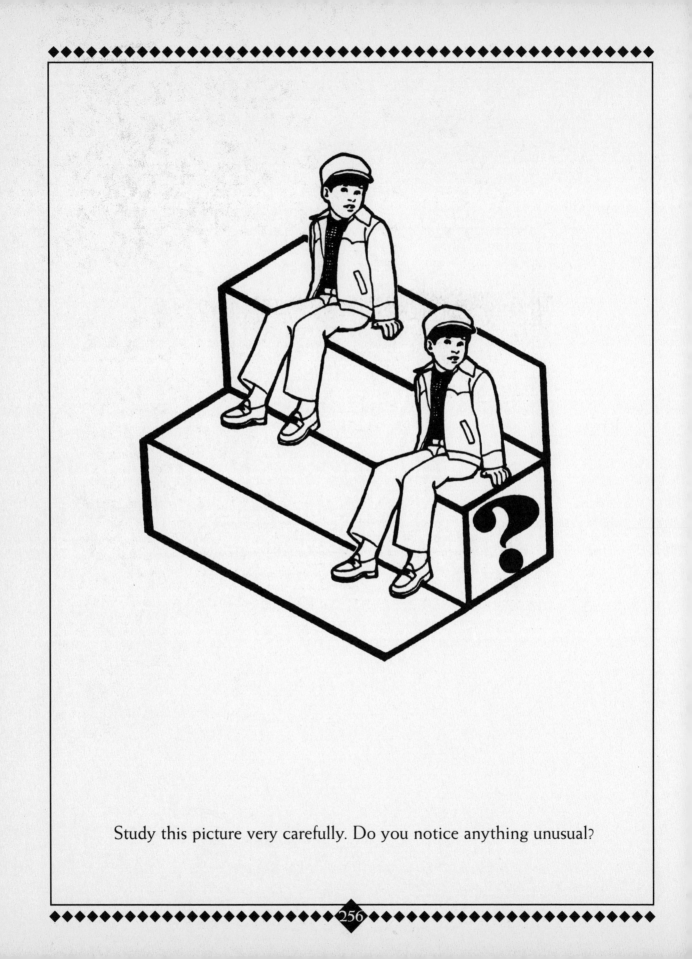

Study this picture very carefully. Do you notice anything unusual?

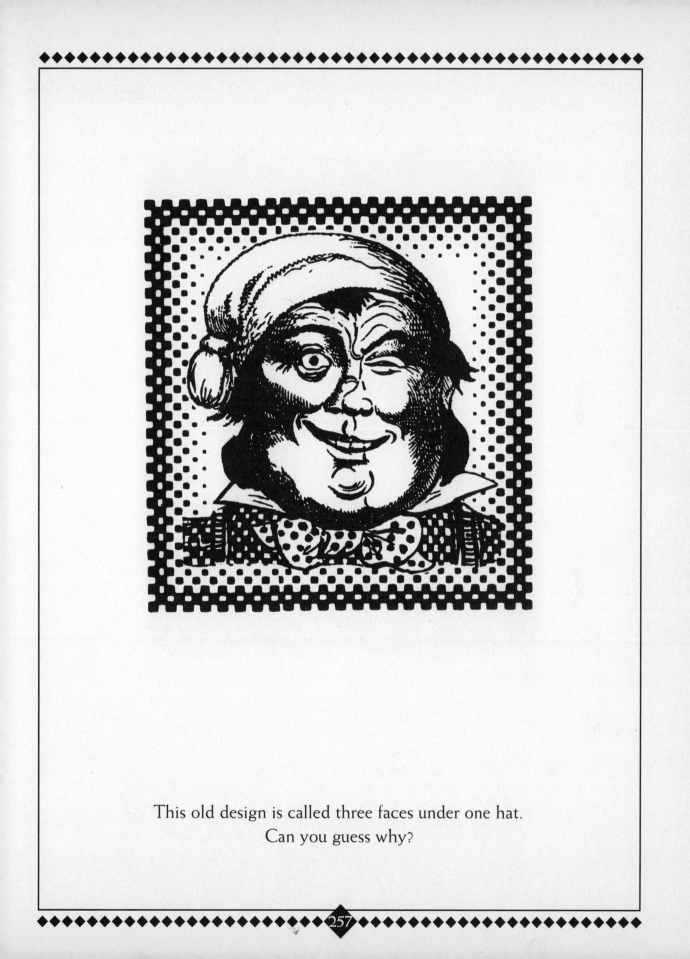

This old design is called three faces under one hat.
Can you guess why?

This lady went on a diet. Examine the picture very carefully. Can you see what she looked like at the end of her diet?

Can you figure out what this set of abstract symbols represents?

Place a pencil along the line of the two arrows. What happens to the color of the wheel?

Can you see what's wrong with this poster?

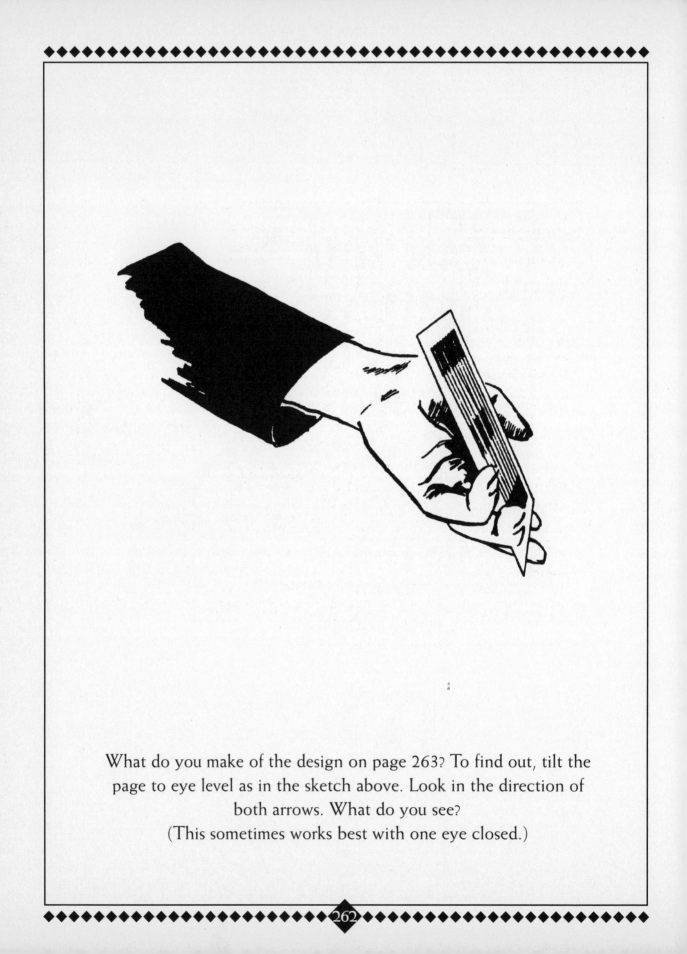

What do you make of the design on page 263? To find out, tilt the page to eye level as in the sketch above. Look in the direction of both arrows. What do you see?

(This sometimes works best with one eye closed.)

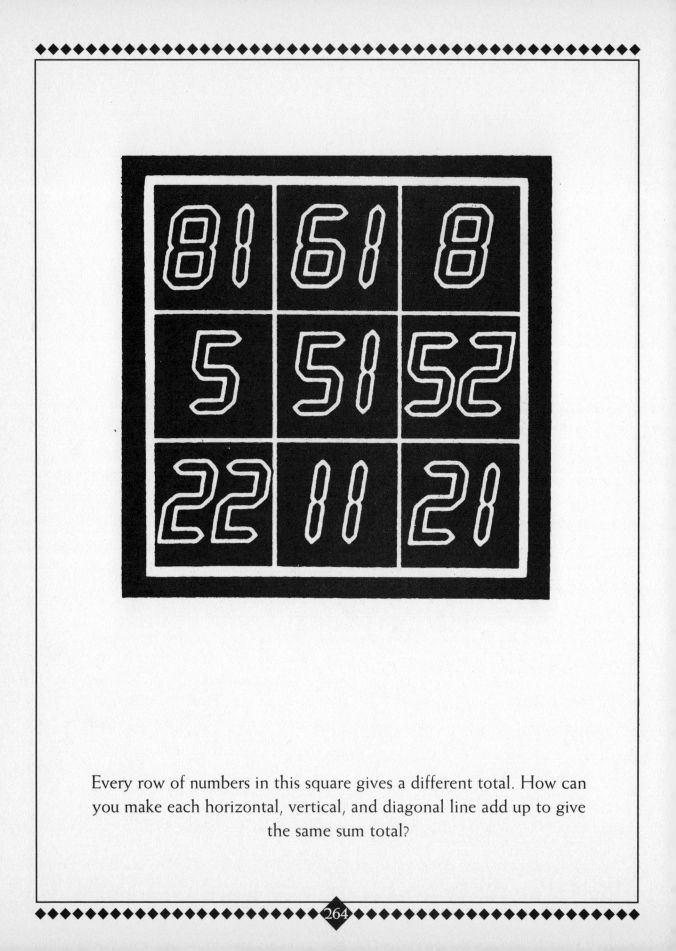

Every row of numbers in this square gives a different total. How can you make each horizontal, vertical, and diagonal line add up to give the same sum total?

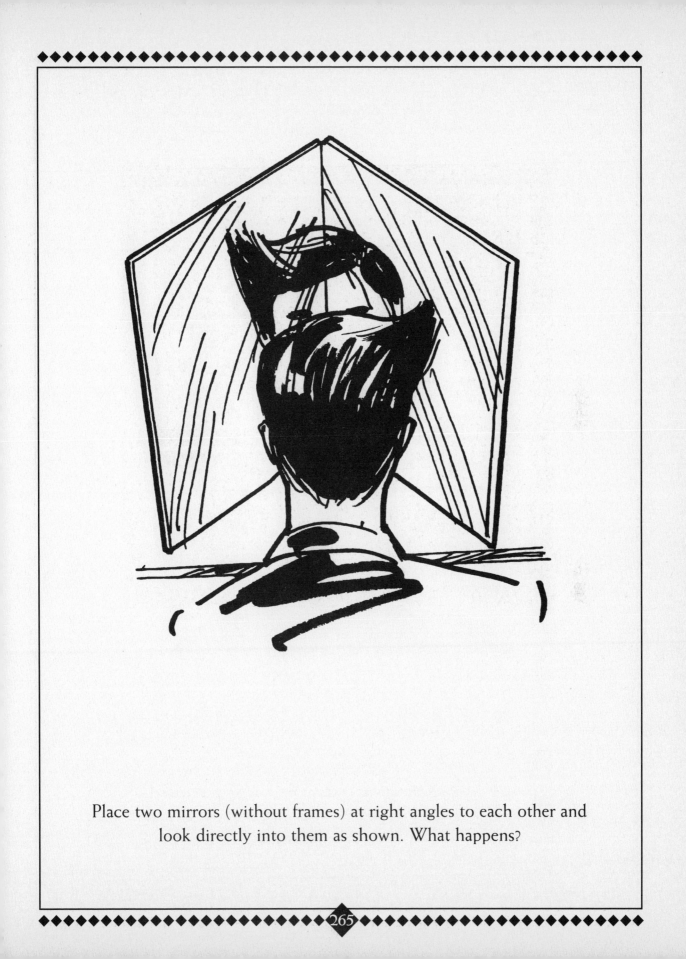

Place two mirrors (without frames) at right angles to each other and look directly into them as shown. What happens?

What do you see? Two people looking at each other or a fancy vase?

Can you discover why this old British colonial patriotic design is
called "The Glory of a Lion Is His Mane"?

Carefully look at this playing card.
Can you figure out which distance is greater,
A–B or B–C?

Stare at this rabbit design without blinking for about 30 seconds
under a bright light. Now look at a blank wall or a piece
of white paper. What do you see?

There are ten small variations in Picture "b." Can you spot them?

Examine this bowl of fruit. Can you find the gardener?

This picture is based on a Victorian "Fantasy Face"—love of the clown. What do you see in this print?

These two boys are afraid of the giant, yet he is hiding
in the picture. Can you find him?

TOO HOT TO HOOT

This phrase is known as a palindrome. It reads the same backwards and forwards. There is something unusual about it. Can you figure it out?

Which of these two bulls looks the larger?

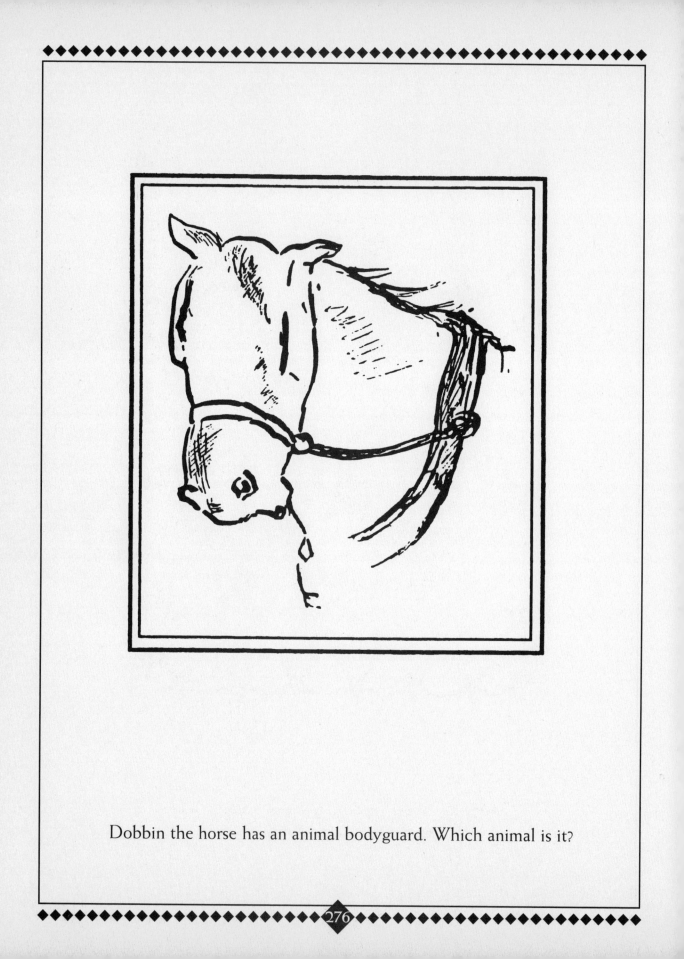

Dobbin the horse has an animal bodyguard. Which animal is it?

Keep staring at this design under a bright light.
After a while, what do you see?

Which dot is the larger?

Can you unearth what these shapes represent?

Hold this page at arm's length. Now slowly bring the page towards your face. What happens to the two birds?

The girl has a thermometer in her mouth. Her temperature is 98.6.
What is unusual about this number?

Does this picture frame get narrower as it gets towards the top?

Look at the girl on this swing. Which looks longer, the upright or
the horizontal bar?

What do you see in this picture?

How many cubes are there in this sketch?

There are five mistakes on this playing card. Can you see them?

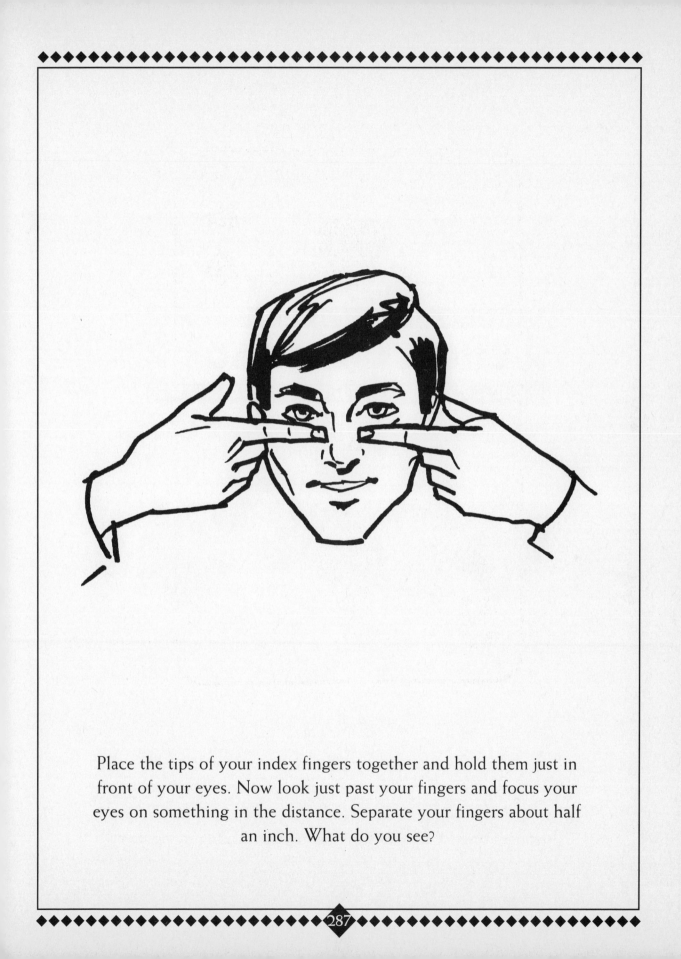

Place the tips of your index fingers together and hold them just in front of your eyes. Now look just past your fingers and focus your eyes on something in the distance. Separate your fingers about half an inch. What do you see?

CHOICE DICE 50¢

The shop was selling poor-quality dice at 50¢ each. This was not the correct price. Can you work out what was the true price?

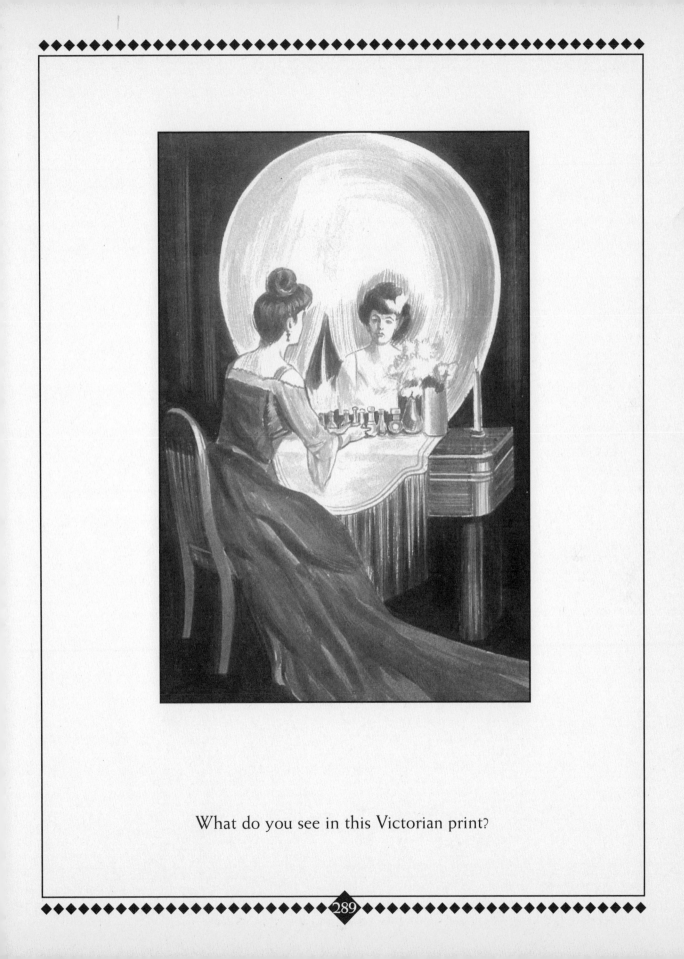

What do you see in this Victorian print?

This innocent-looking boy is very mischievous. He has a cheeky pet animal too. What is it?

Look at the intersections of the white lines. What do you see?

Are these real circles?

Very slowly read the words on the front of the box.
What does it say?

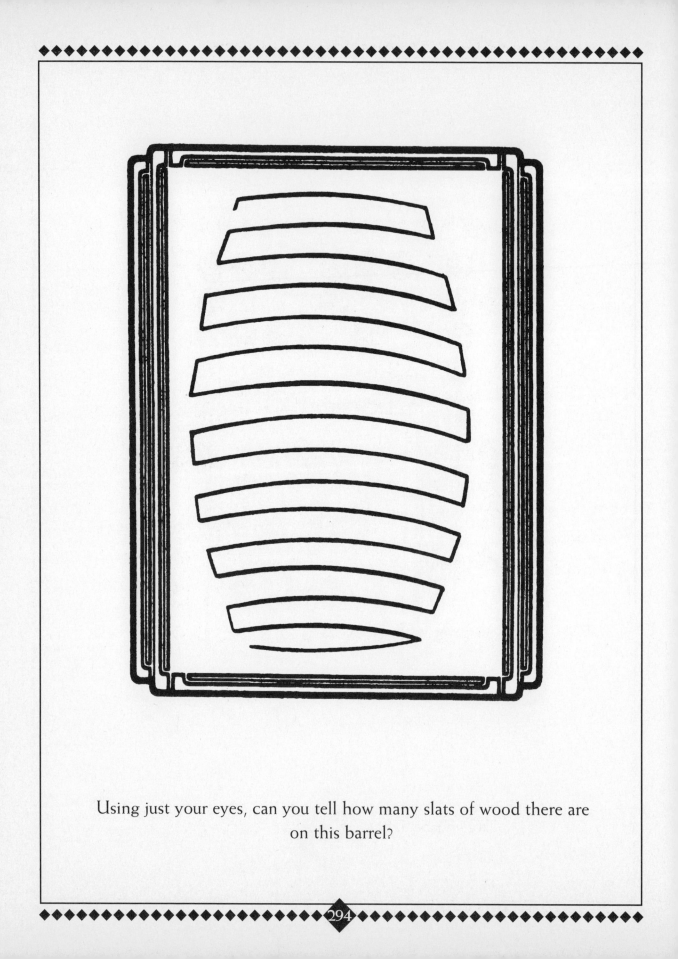

Using just your eyes, can you tell how many slats of wood there are on this barrel?

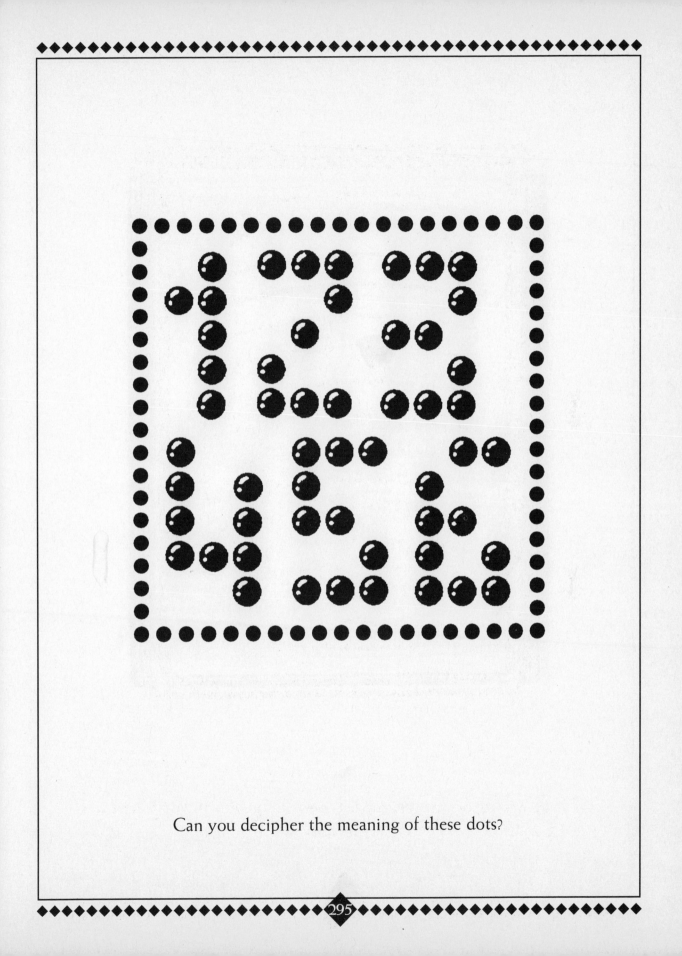

Can you decipher the meaning of these dots?

The soldiers are looking for the spy, but they can't find him.
Can you?

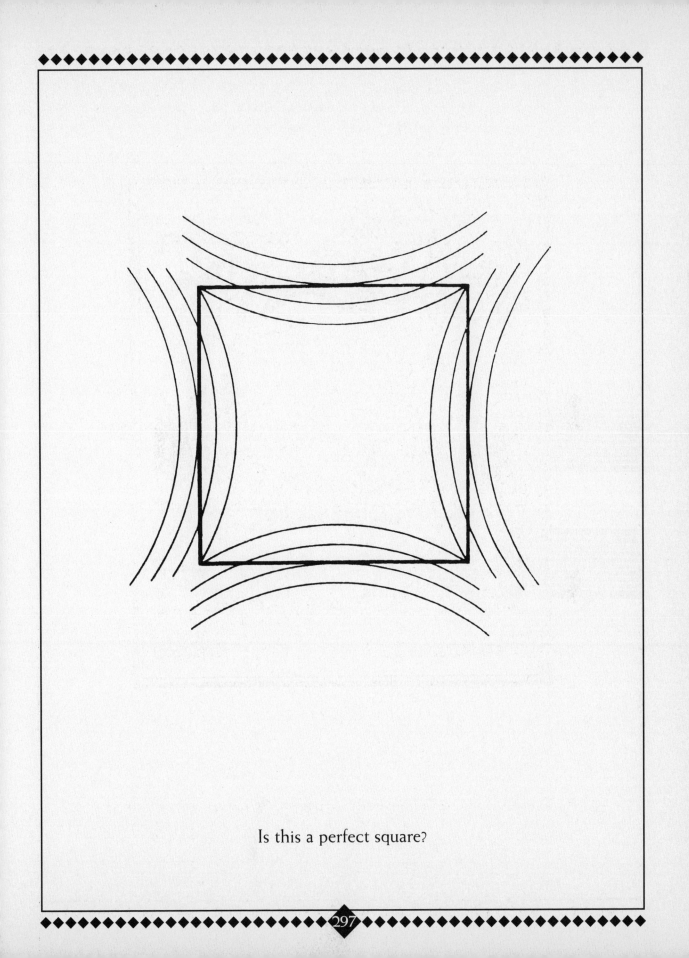

Is this a perfect square?

Is this set of squares pointing up to the left or down to the right?

Why is this picture called "The Lady of the Lake"?

What is the meaning of this set of letters?

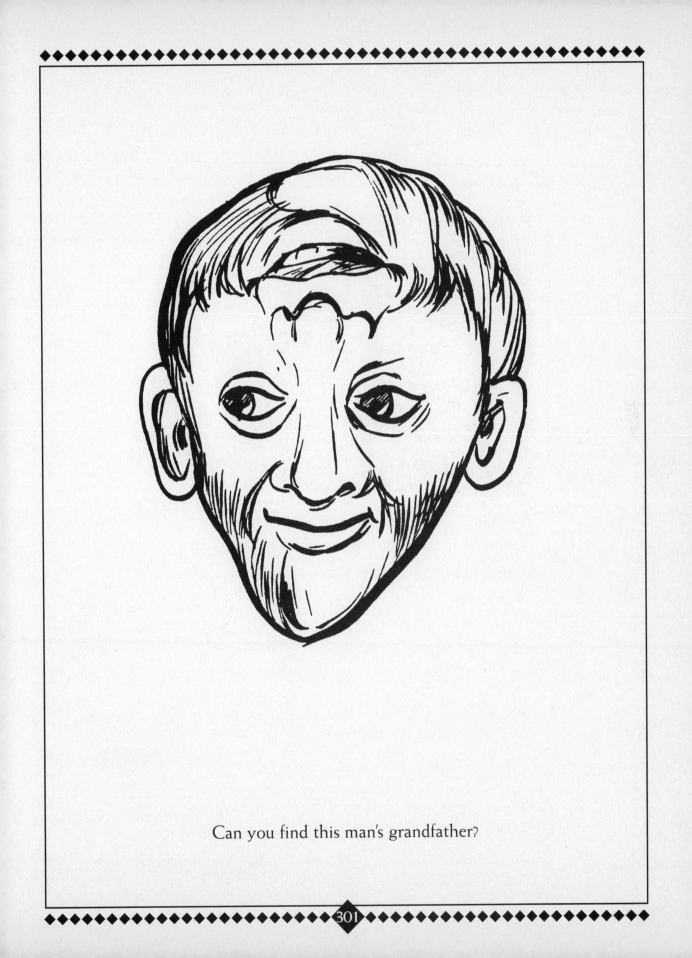

Can you find this man's grandfather?

**KID GLOVES
DICE GAMBLE
BEECH NUTS
CHOICE QUALITY
COOKBOOK PAGES**

Turn this page upside down and look at its reflection in a mirror.
What strange thing occurs when you do this?

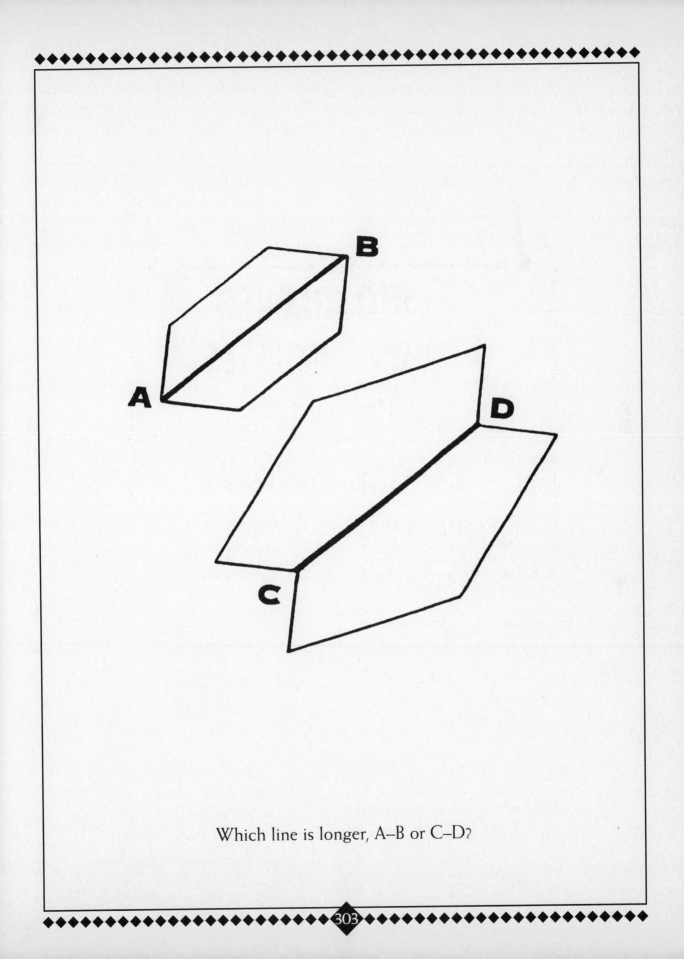

Which line is longer, A–B or C–D?

THE MAGIC SPINNER

Photocopy this page onto a piece of thin card. Cut it out and rotate
it as shown on the opposite page.
What do you see spinning in the disk?

What will happen if you draw a square on a balloon with a ballpoint pen and then blow the balloon up? Can you figure out what the square will look like?

Can you discover this secret word?

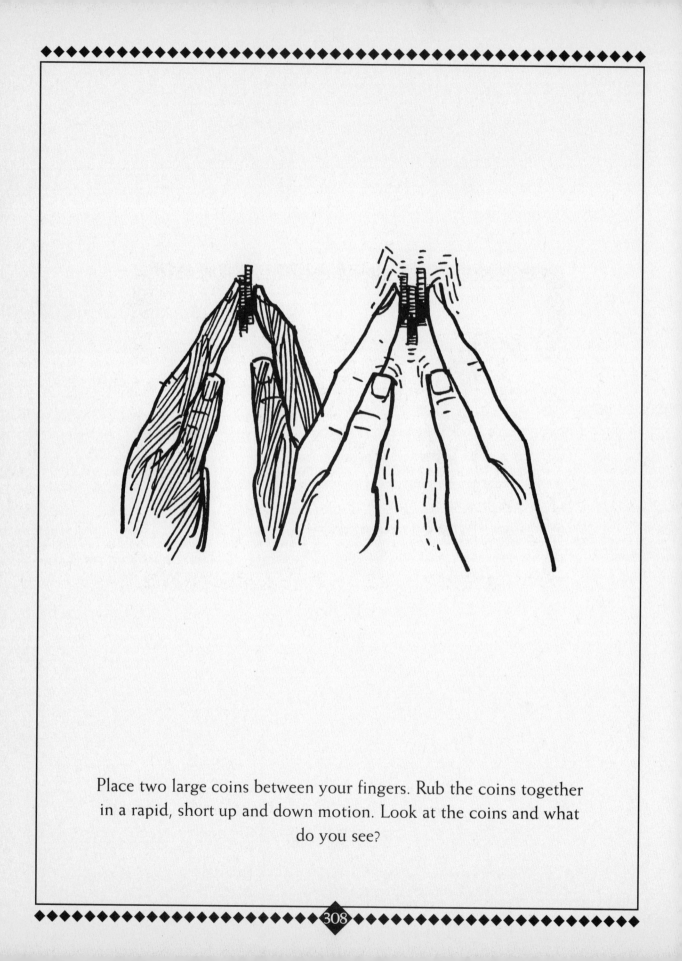

Place two large coins between your fingers. Rub the coins together in a rapid, short up and down motion. Look at the coins and what do you see?

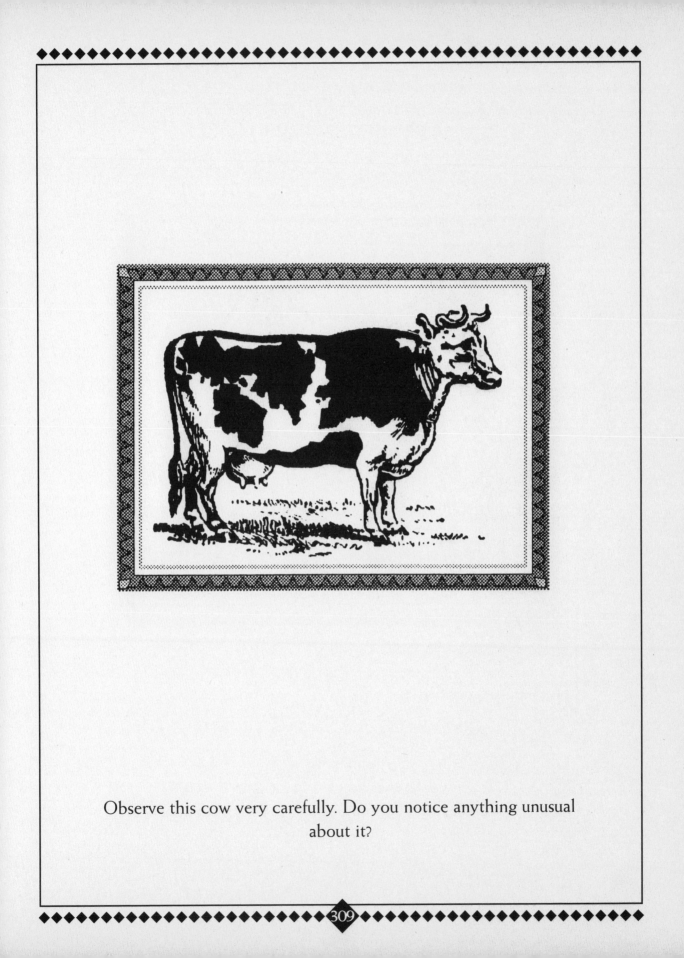

Observe this cow very carefully. Do you notice anything unusual about it?

The shepherd is playing his flute. Can you find him hidden in this picture?

Can you work out what these shapes represent?

Put a bright postage stamp on the table and cover it with a glass of
water. Now place a saucer on top of the glass.
What happens to the stamp?

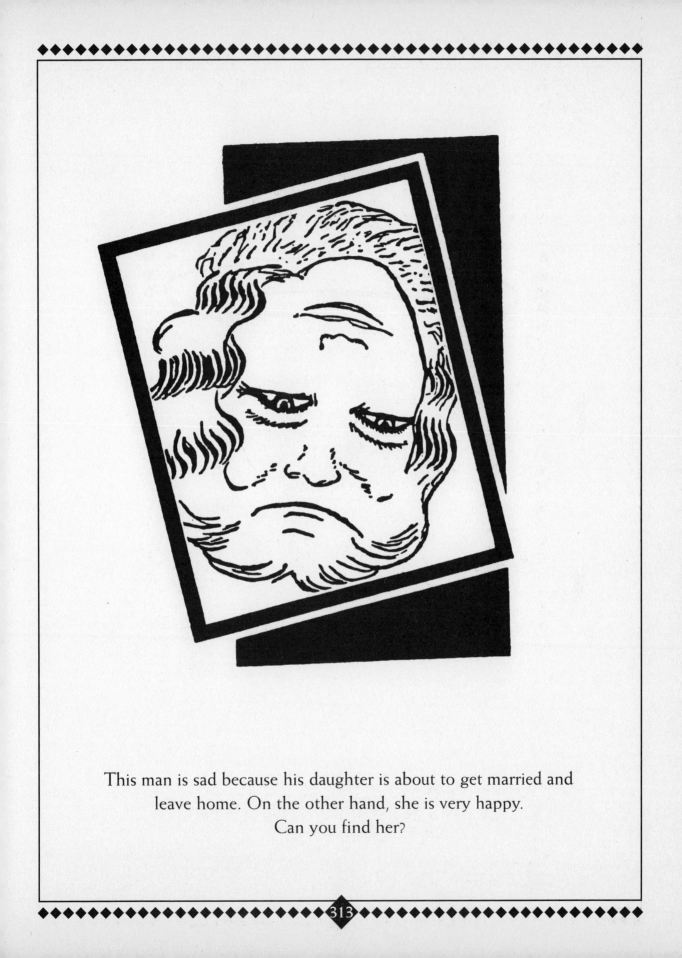

This man is sad because his daughter is about to get married and leave home. On the other hand, she is very happy. Can you find her?

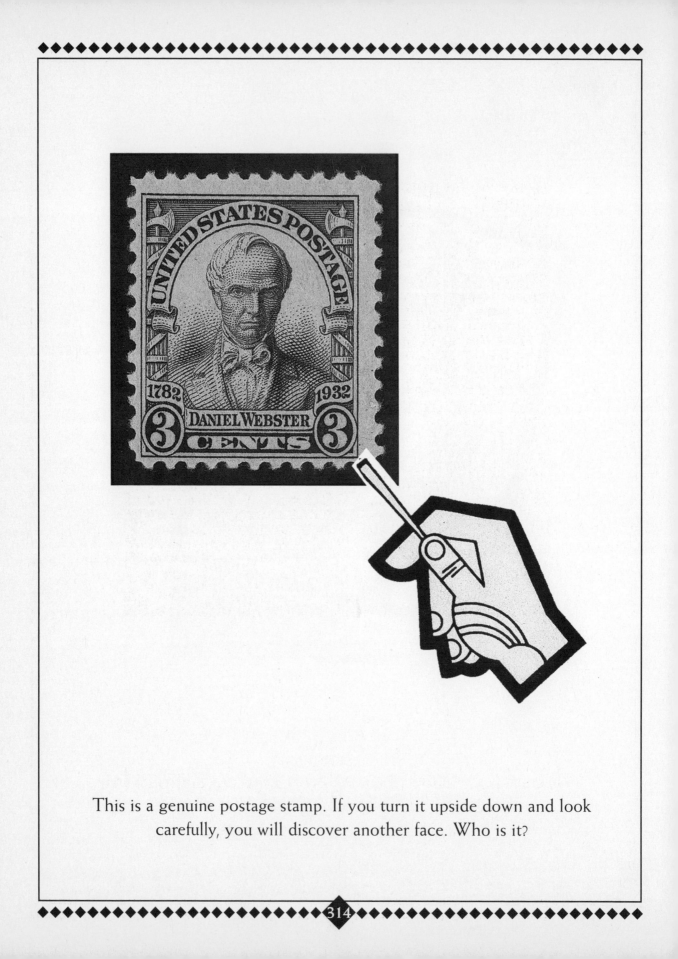

This is a genuine postage stamp. If you turn it upside down and look carefully, you will discover another face. Who is it?

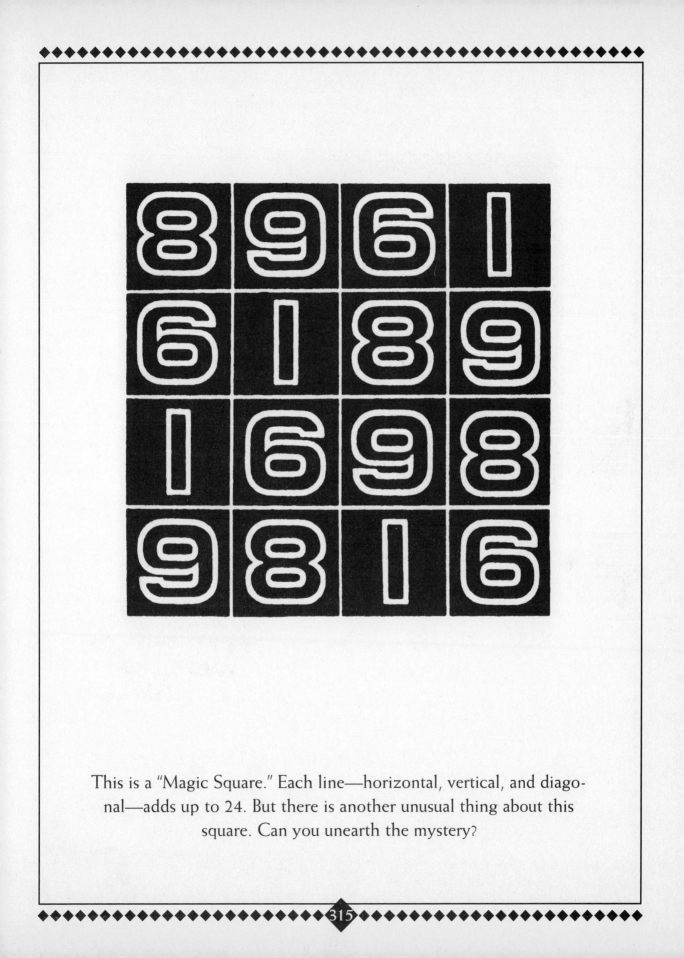

This is a "Magic Square." Each line—horizontal, vertical, and diagonal—adds up to 24. But there is another unusual thing about this square. Can you unearth the mystery?

How can you get the bird to fly into the snake's mouth?

Is Side "a" of the illustration high or is Side "b"?

Stare at this picture without blinking for about 30 seconds. Now turn your gaze onto a blank wall or sheet of white paper. A mystery figure will appear. Do you recognize him?

Can you work out what these shapes represent?

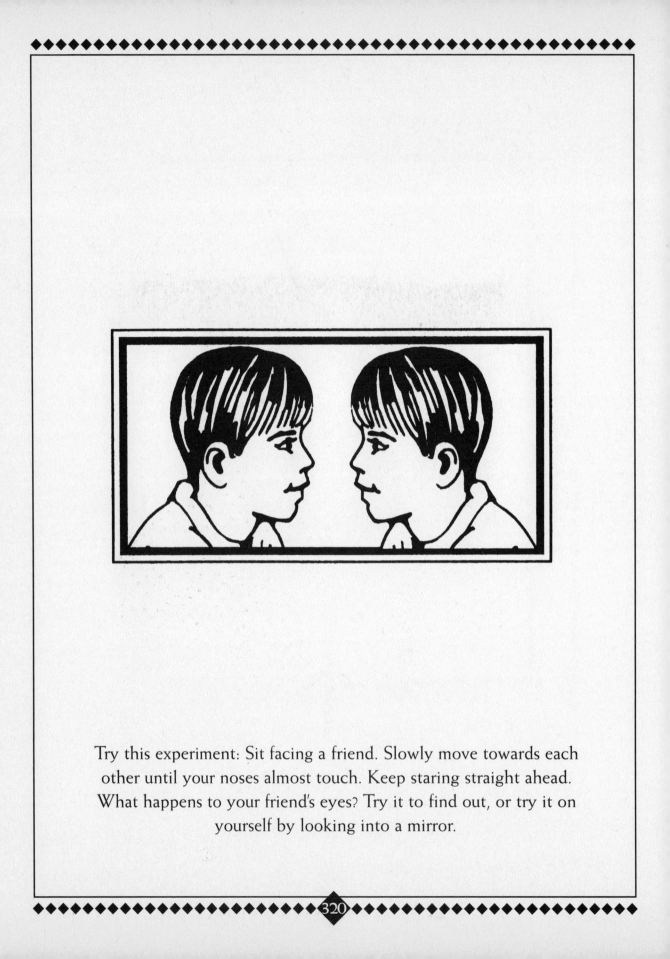

Try this experiment: Sit facing a friend. Slowly move towards each other until your noses almost touch. Keep staring straight ahead. What happens to your friend's eyes? Try it to find out, or try it on yourself by looking into a mirror.

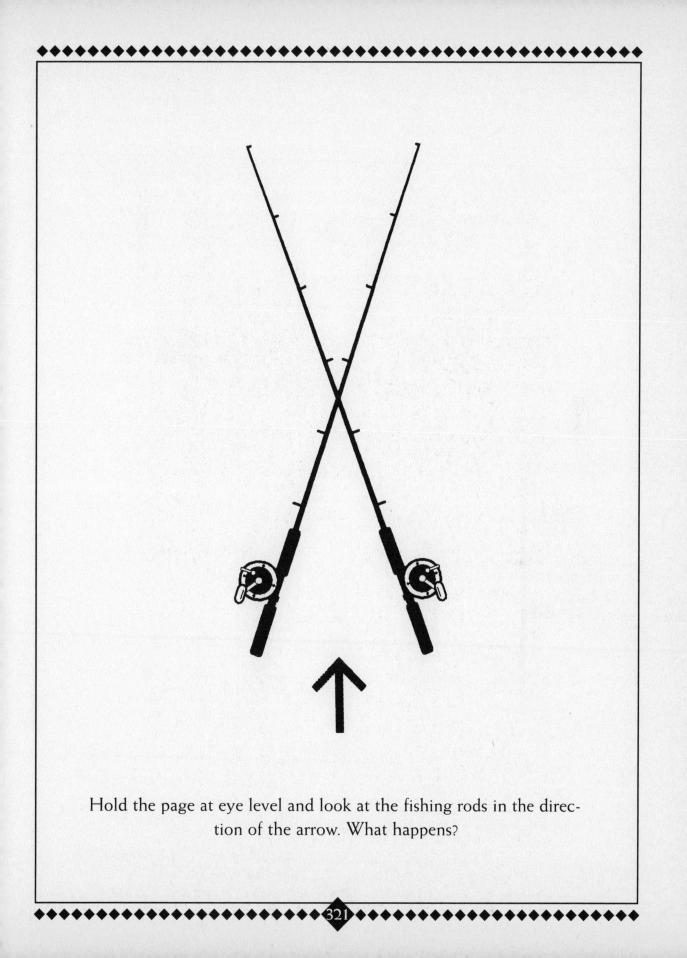

Hold the page at eye level and look at the fishing rods in the direction of the arrow. What happens?

Another design from times past. This British soldier is happy because the enemy is on the run. Who is the enemy?

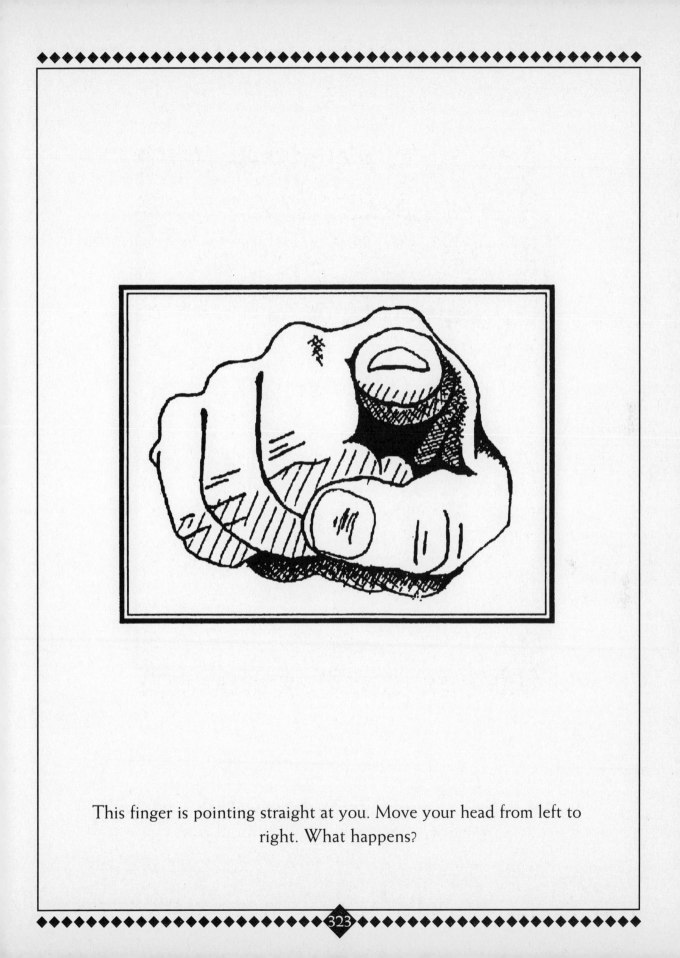

This finger is pointing straight at you. Move your head from left to right. What happens?

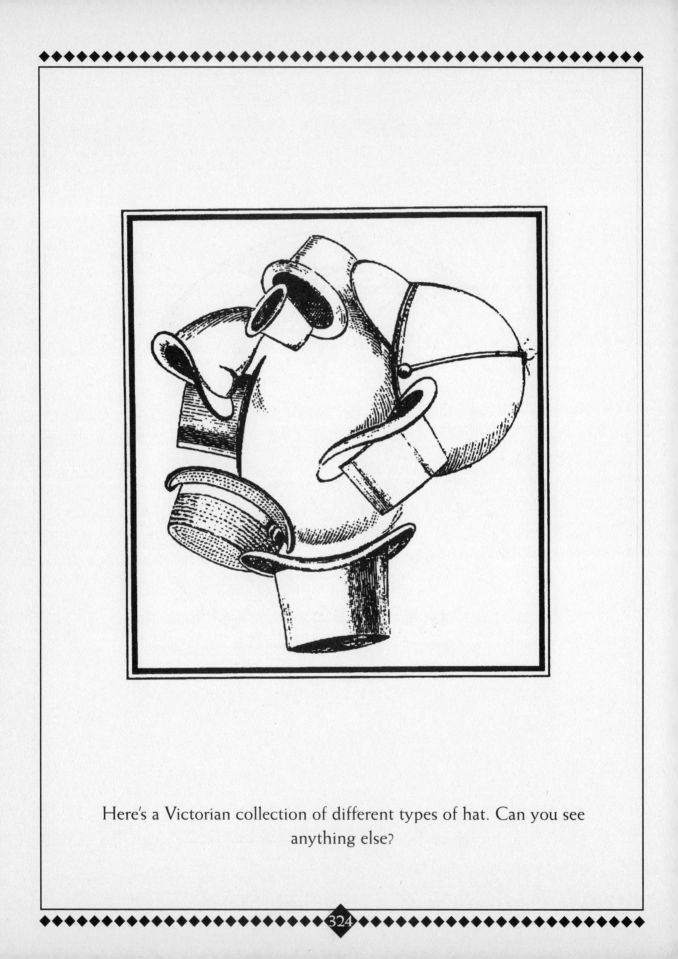

Here's a Victorian collection of different types of hat. Can you see
anything else?

Which of these two dots is in the true center?

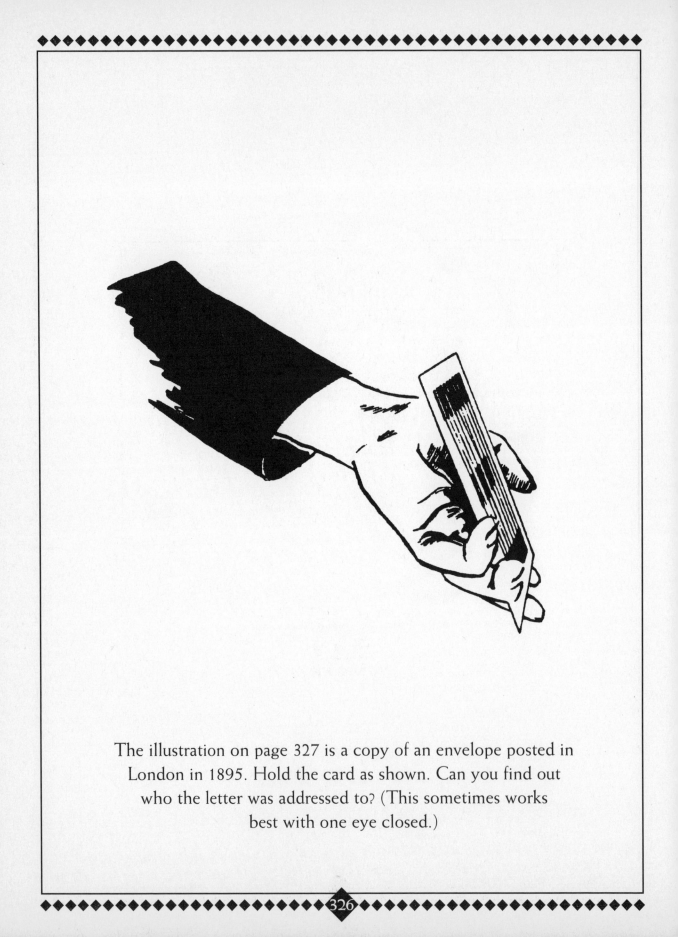

The illustration on page 327 is a copy of an envelope posted in London in 1895. Hold the card as shown. Can you find out who the letter was addressed to? (This sometimes works best with one eye closed.)

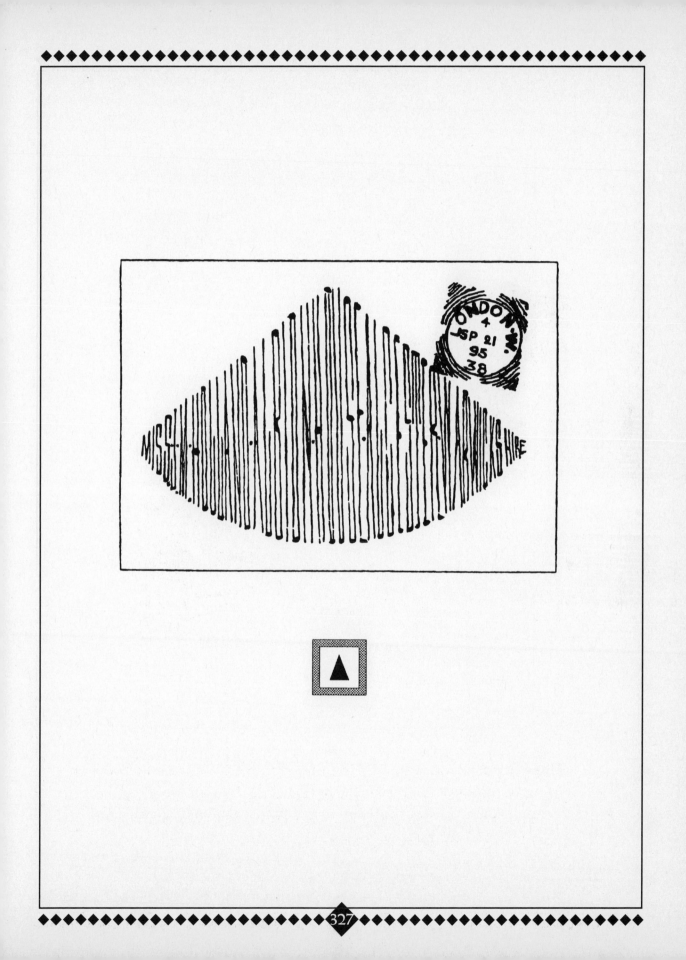

The original artwork for this print is called "Tête du Mort" (Head of Death). Why do you think it was given this title?

Bring the page slowly towards your face. What happens?

Stare at these diagonal lines for a while. What do you see?

The farmer's son was adding up the large number of eggs laid over a 3-week period. Do you see anything unusual with the answer?

Read the words on this notice board very slowly to yourself.
What does it say?

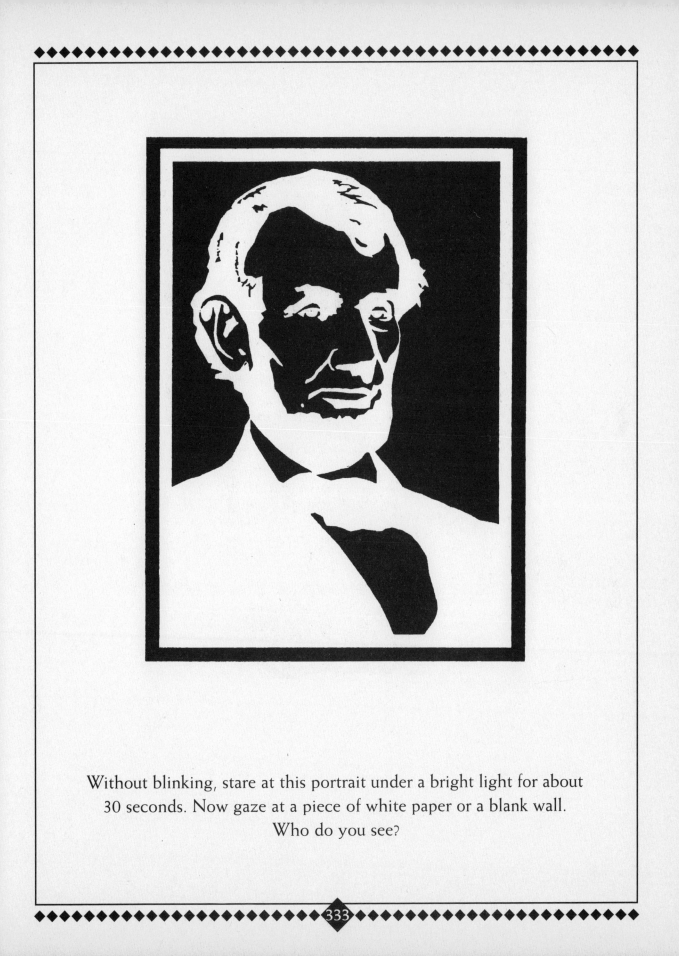

Without blinking, stare at this portrait under a bright light for about 30 seconds. Now gaze at a piece of white paper or a blank wall. Who do you see?

What is this creature, a rabbit or a duck?

Can you see what is unusual about this mysterious old lady?

Where is the master of this faithful horse?

Slowly rotate this page in a circular motion.
What happens to the clown's balloon?

Which square is the wider and which one is the taller?

This design is made up from straight lines. Look at it for a while
and you may see other shapes. What are they?

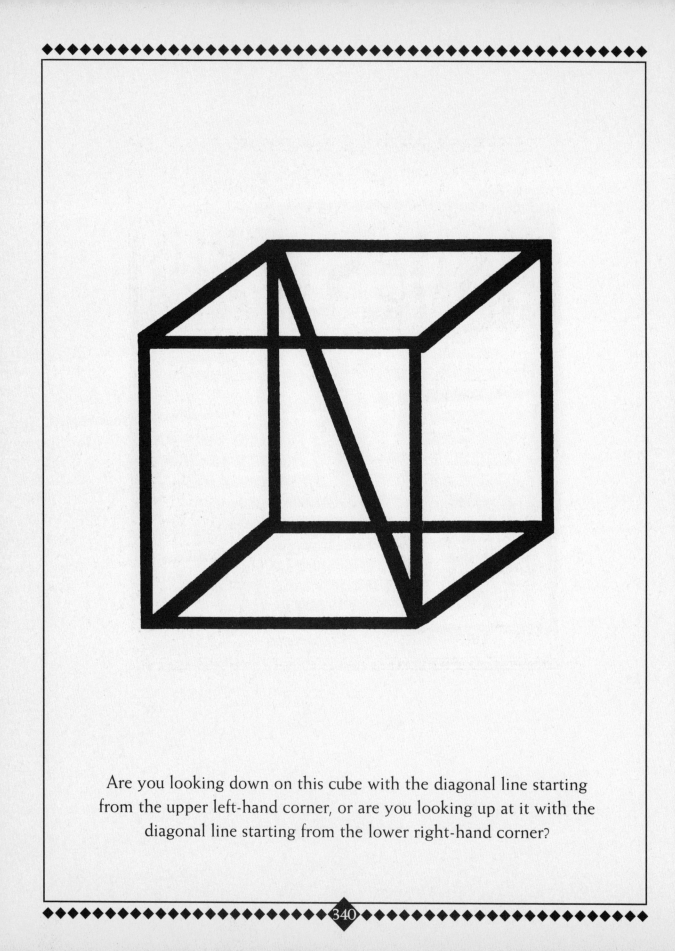

Are you looking down on this cube with the diagonal line starting from the upper left-hand corner, or are you looking up at it with the diagonal line starting from the lower right-hand corner?

In this woodland scene two giants are searching for a girl. Can you
find all three in this picture?

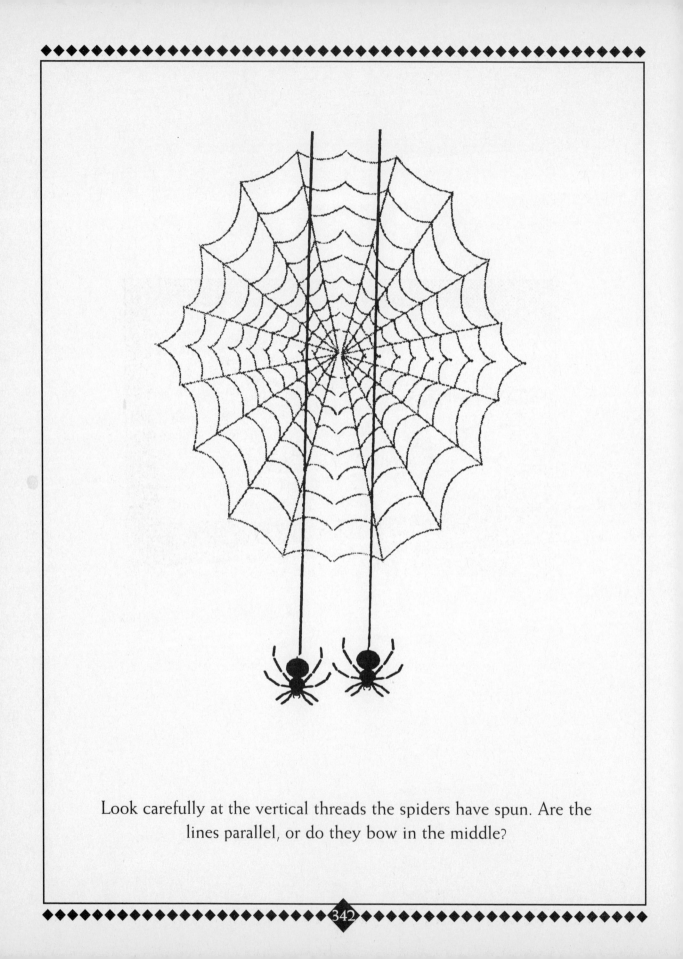

Look carefully at the vertical threads the spiders have spun. Are the lines parallel, or do they bow in the middle?

The number 96 is not 69 upside down. Can you explain?

Look at this frame very carefully. Does it bulge out in the center?

Can you spot anything unusual about this bearded man?

Are you looking down a tunnel or are you on top of a
pyramid looking downwards?

Can you find the man of the mountain?

Can you figure out the significance of the numbers beneath
Napoleon's portrait?

How many children can you see in this vintage etching?

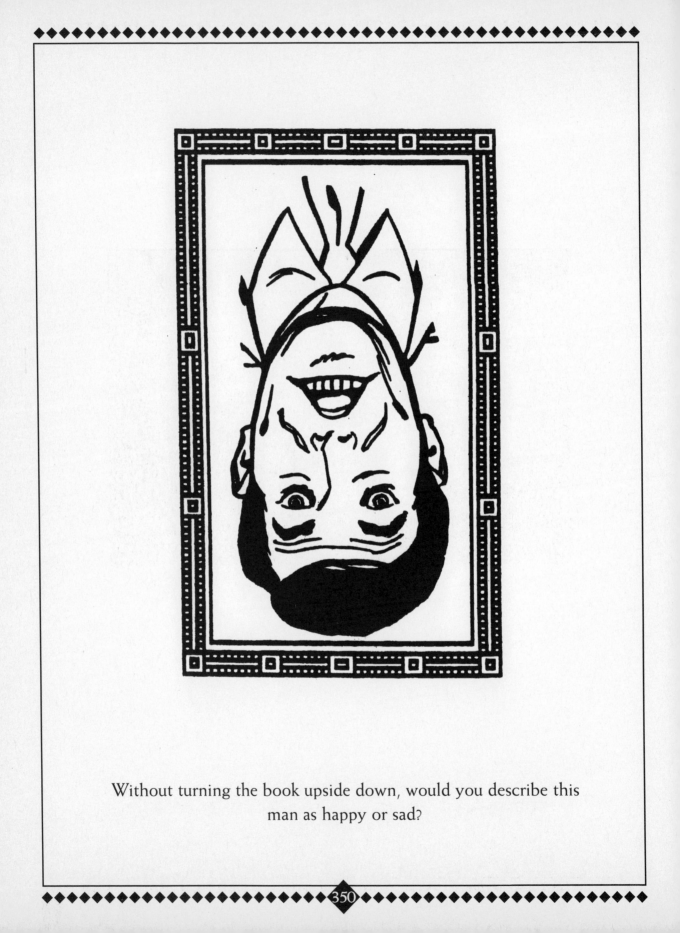

Without turning the book upside down, would you describe this man as happy or sad?

What animals do we have here, two ducks or two rabbits?

How would you describe this illustration? Is it a black square with four small white squares inside, or is it four black arrows pointing out to each corner?

This is another sketch from World War I. Can you find the kaiser hiding in this tiger design?

Can you find Santa Claus in this quaint Christmas scene?

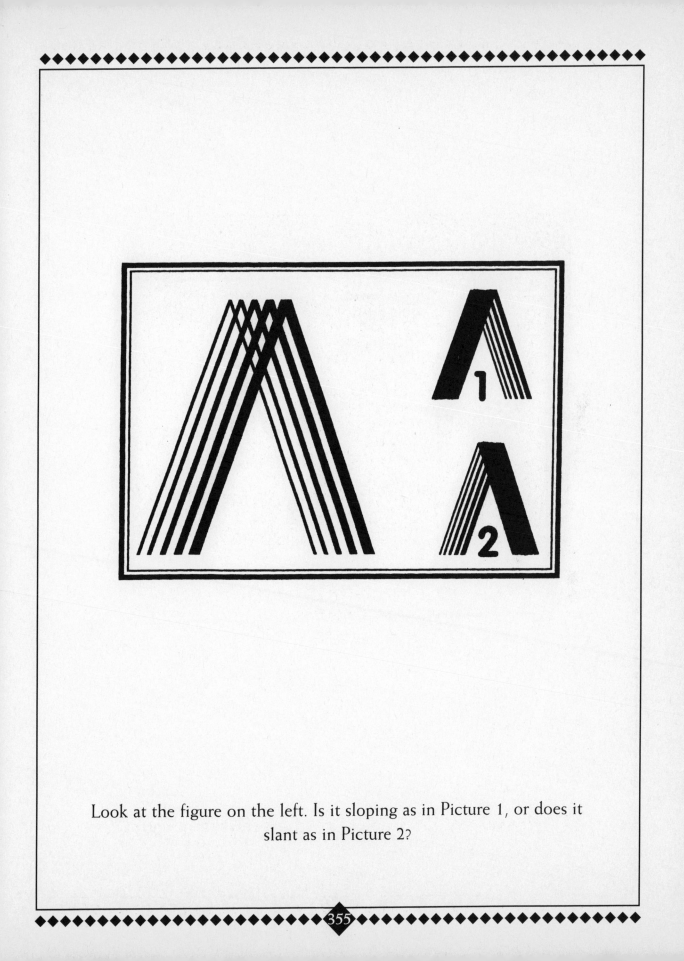

Look at the figure on the left. Is it sloping as in Picture 1, or does it slant as in Picture 2?

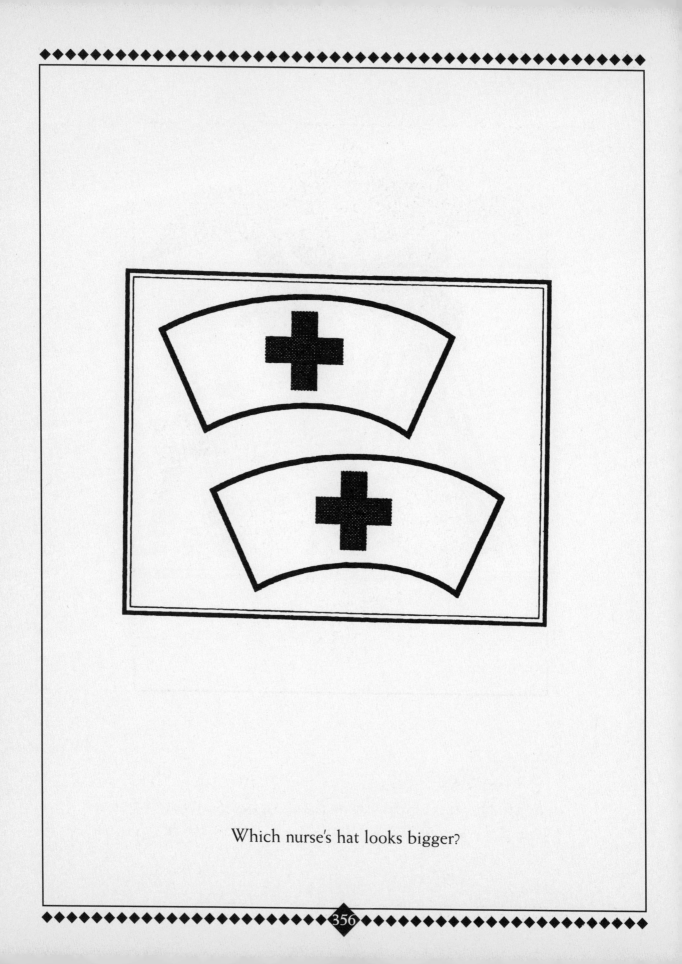

Which nurse's hat looks bigger?

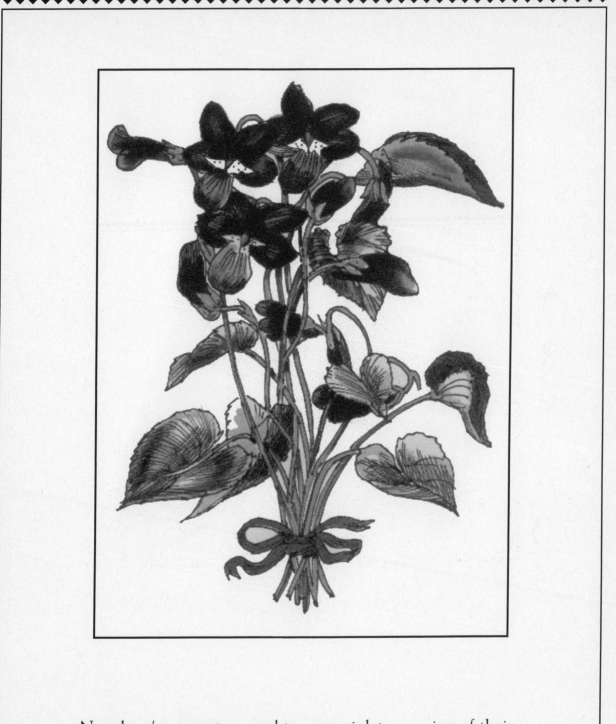

Napoleon's supporters used to wear violets as a sign of their allegiance. This print hides the faces of Napoleon, Maria Louisa, and the young King of Rome. Can you find them?

What do you see, the head of a Native American or an
Eskimo looking into a cave?

The
Answers

Page 8: Illusion. This is an impossible creation.

Page 10: Never. This is a trick drawing.

Page 11: There is no way to tell. The twin with the horizontal stripes seems to be fatter, but he really isn't. Our eyes follow the lines in his suit, so the twin on the right seems broader and shorter than his brother.

Page 12: No, but it seems higher and wider in the back because of the way it has been drawn. We expect the back of it to be farther away and to look smaller. Since it is the same size, we automatically assume it is bigger in the back.

Page 13, top: Both are possible. It depends on how you look at it.

Page 13, bottom: No. But it seems to be, because "b" is in a larger area.

Page 14: They are all the same height. The man at the right looks tallest. We expect things to look smaller when they are farther away. The man at the right is farthest away and we would expect him to look the smallest. Since he doesn't, we assume he's really larger than the others.

Page 15: The dot-shaped cross is just to the right of the center of the diagram. It spells out "R-I-G-H-T." It may take you a while to find it because the other dots distract your attention.

Page 16, top: They are the same length. Our eyes follow the lines. The "a" line seems to expand because of the "wings" on the ends. Line "b" is cut off by its arrowheads, so it looks shorter.

Page 16, bottom: Exactly. They seem longer in relation to their sur-roundings.

Pages 17–21:

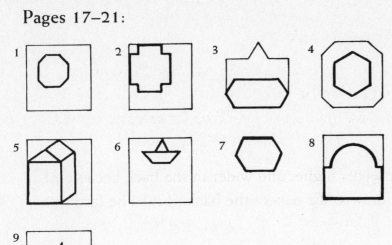

Page 22: A triangle with equal sides.

Page 23, top: They are all the same size.

Page 23, bottom: Line "a" equals "b" and "c" equals "d." Line "a" seems longer than "b" because we unconsciously add the circles on the end of the line to it's length. The same is true of line "c" with its open square.

Page 24: In "a" — both are the same size, but the white one seems larger. When bright light falls on the retina of our eyes (where the nerve cells are), more nerve fibres react than had actually been hit by the light. This causes a "spreading effect," and the light object seems larger than it actually is. In "b," the black circle is actually larger, although both seem to be the same size.

Page 25: Each egg fits into all the egg cups.

Pages 26 and 27: The inner circles are the same size. The one on the right looks smaller because we usually judge the size of an object by contrasting it with the objects around it.

Pages 28 and 29: Both gray areas have the same intensity. The white lines make the area on the left seem brighter.

Page 30, top: Measure it. The curved lines force our eyes to move to the left of the true center.

Page 30, bottom: It is exactly in the center.

Page 31, top: The cross-bars are exactly in the center of the triangles.

Page 31, bottom: No, they are both the same size. This is another example of the difficulty of judging size when angles are involved.

Page 32: Both circles are the same size. The arrows pull our eyes inward in the top circle, and our eyes follow the arrows outward in the lower one.

Page 33: All the objects are the same length.

Page 36: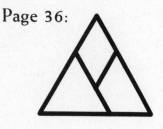

Page 37: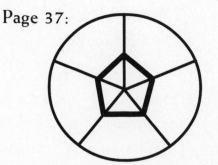

Page 38: No. To best visualize her path, let's undo the cube into its component flattened faces. From this diagram, you can see that the shortest distance between two points is a straight line. That line does not coincide with her planned path (shown as a dotted line).

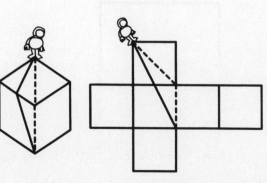

Page 39:

Page 39, bottom:

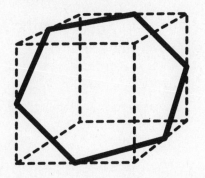

Page 40: Just open the bottom link. The top two links are not attached to each other.

Page 41: It will come free of the pipe. To visualize this action, start at the pipe. From there, trace the pipe's path out from the center. After a few turns, the pipe exits freely at the opening on the right side of the maze.

Page 42:

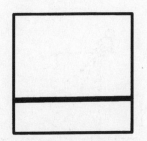

Page 43: Part I: Twenty-two sides. Part II: Thirty-six sides.

Page 44: C.

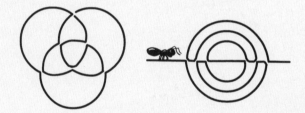

cube not
shown

Page 45, top: B is the only pattern that will produce a four-sided triangular pyramid.

Page 45, bottom: Six. At every half hour of the journey, you'll pass an incoming train. If you count the inbound train in the Metropolis station and don't count the inbound train in the Gotham City station, you'll pass six trains.

Page 46: 27 triangles: 16 one-cell triangles, 7 four-cell triangles, 3 nine-cell triangles, and 1 sixteen-cell triangle.

Page 47:

Page 48: Eighteen, but you don't have to trace out each one. The easiest way to solve this puzzle is to start at the beginning and determine the number of paths that can get you to an intersection. The number of paths to each successive intersection is equal to the sum of the paths that are "attached" to it.

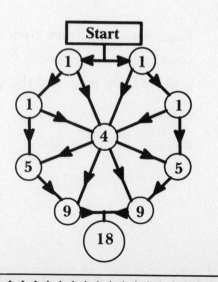

Page 49, top: 21. As you move clockwise around the circle, the number on each section is equal to the sum of the two previous sections.

Page 49, bottom: Fifteen handshakes. The first person would have shaken hands five times. The next person only needed to make four handshakes, since the handshake with one person had already been completed. The next person required only three, and so on. That gives us $5+4+3+2+1=15$.

Page 50: E.

Page 51: 56 pages. Here's how the numbers are arranged on each double sheet.

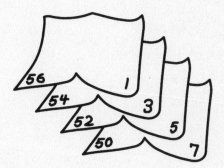

Page 52: Cubes A and D.

Page 53: Pattern D.

Page 54, top: Since they have the same number of teeth, they will spin at the same speed. Cog C does not affect the rate of teeth passage; it only transfers the passage of teeth from cog B to cog D.

Page 54, bottom: The bottom-row center hand is unlike the others. It alone is a right hand.

Page 55: No, the belts are arranged in a pattern that doesn't allow them to move.

Page 56: D.

Page 57: The dial arrow located in the middle of the bottom row is most unusual. In contrast to the rest, it has two heads and only one tail.

Page 60:

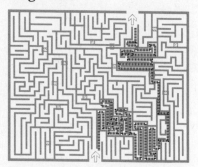

Page 61:

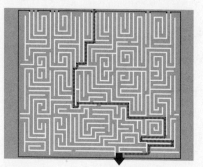

Page 62:

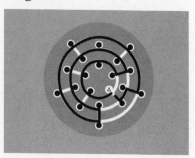

Page 64:

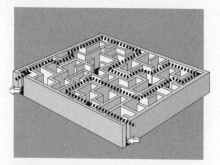

Page 65:

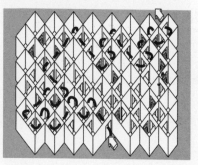

Page 66:

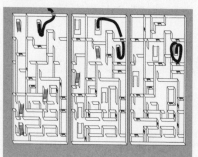

Page 67:

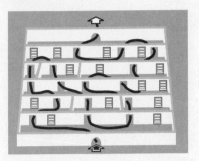

Page 68:

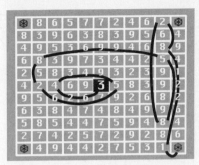

Page 69:

Page 71:

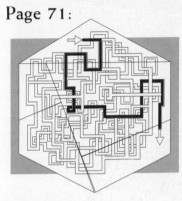

Page 72:

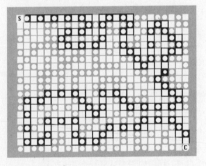

Page 73:

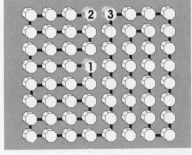

Page 76: It depends on which you saw first—the horizontal A, B, C, or the verticle 12, 13, 14.

Page 77: The ball appears to spin around!

Page 78: You see a black skull in a white frame.

Page 79: The three donkeys have only three ears between them!

Page 80: Either one. The design reverses.

Page 81: Look at the left-hand side of the picture.

Page 82: Both. The design "flip-flops."

Page 83: The girl feeds the goose.

Page 84: Guess first, and then use a ruler to line up the lines. Yes, it's "Y".

Page 85: First count the flames—5. Now count the base of each candle, and you'll find there are 7.

Page 86: His mouth looks like a bird and his eyes and nose look like a bat.

Page 87: Turn the page upside down to find the answer. It says "Life."

Page 88: Take your pick!

Page 89: Joseph Stalin.

Page 90: Take your pick!

Page 91: Actually, the back wheel has been drawn as an oval shape, to give the picture the correct perspective.

Page 92: This is an example of "closure." Your brain fills in the missing bits.

Page 93: The two cards are the Eight of Clubs and the Queen of Hearts.

Page 94: Between them, these strange fish have only one head.

Page 95: Each tube can be seen to open in different directions.

Page 96: Look closely and you'll find profiles of Adam and Eve.

Page 97: It's an impossible elephant. Look at its legs—can you figure them out?

Page 98: Either one.

Page 99: The bird flies to the perch.

Page 100: Close one eye and bring the other eye close to the page. The checkerboard will straighten out.

Page 101: Turn him upside down.

Pages 102 and 103: You can see this any way you want.

Page 104: The wheels on the bicycle appear to spin and revolve.

Page 105: They are both the same size, but the white one looks larger because darker things seem smaller than lighter ones.

Page 106: Either one—this is another illusion where the design flip-flops.

Page 107: A beggar holding out a hand—or the profile of a goofy face.

Page 108: They are both the same size, but the curves make #1 look larger.

Page 109: No, it's a series of circles within circles. Check it by tracing them with your finger. This illusion is known as the Fraser Spiral.

Page 110: They form an impossible triangle! The idea was first drawn in Sweden in 1934 by Oscar Reutersvard.

Page 111: It depends on how you look at it.

Page 112: Because this pattern can be viewed from either direction, the brain alternates from one view to the other.

Page 113: After you make a guess, use a ruler to check. In this illusion, the outside lines help to convince us that the bottom fish is bigger.

Page 114: To find out, turn the page upside down.

Page 115: Each circle will seem to revolve on its axis. The inner cog wheel will appear to rotate in the opposite direction.

Page 138:

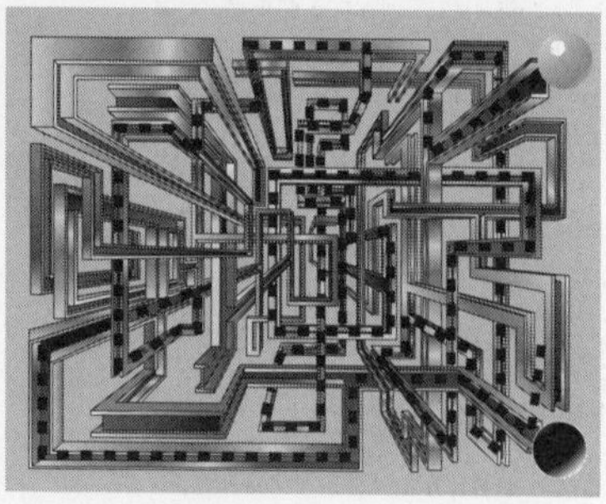

Page 139:

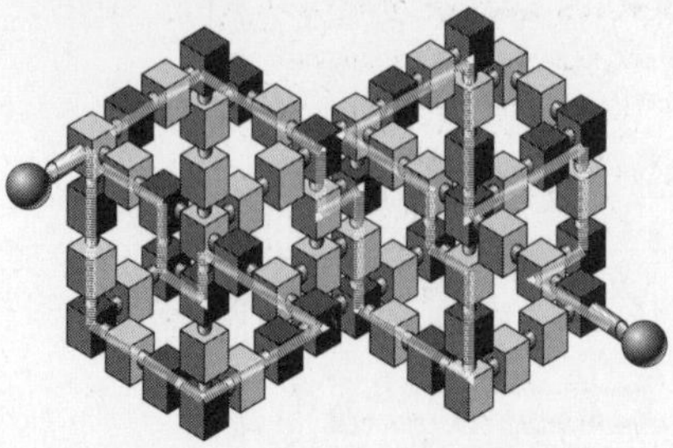

Page 140:

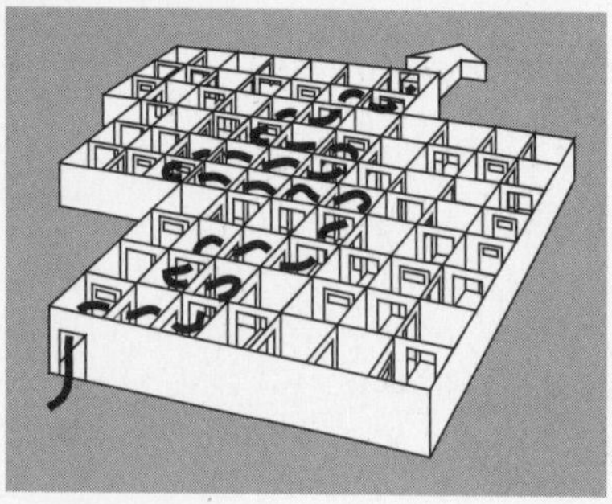

Page 141:

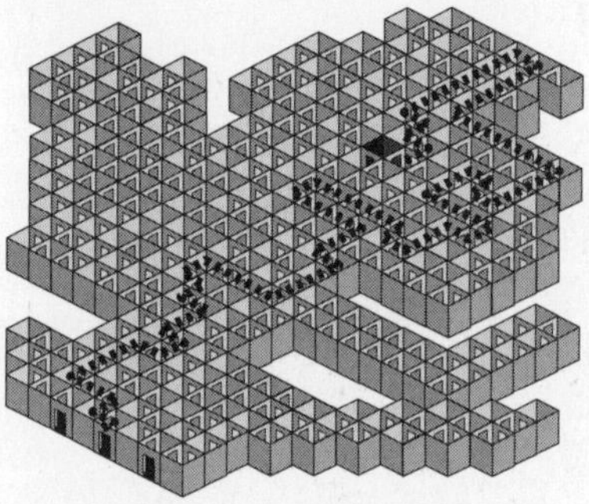

Page 142:

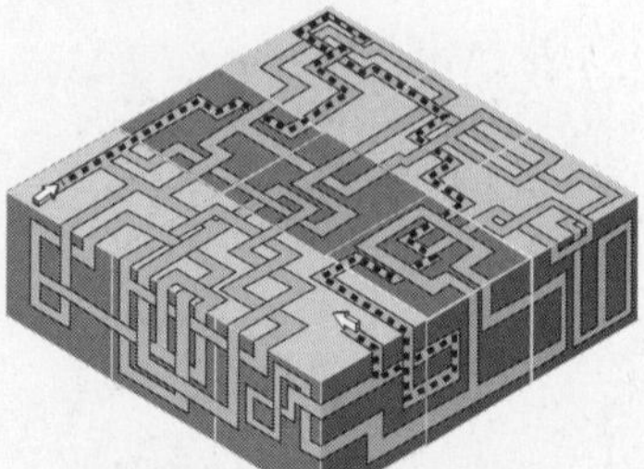

Page 143:

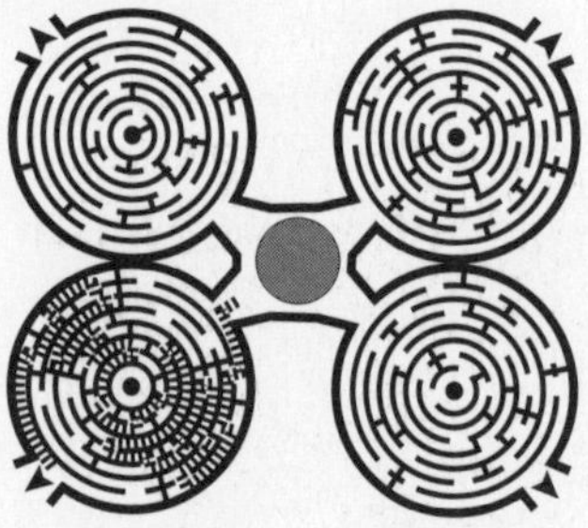

Page 144:

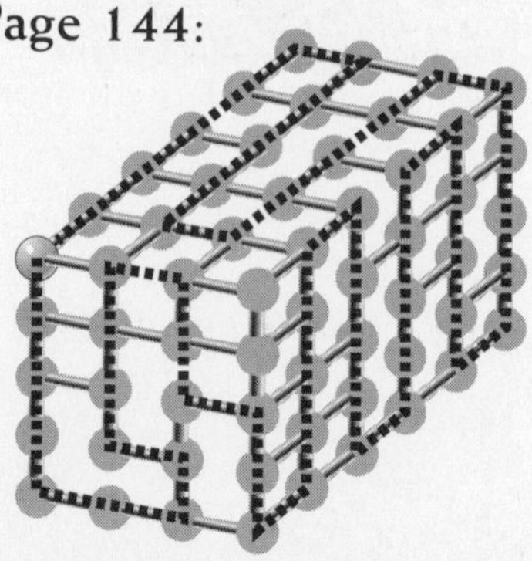

Page 145:

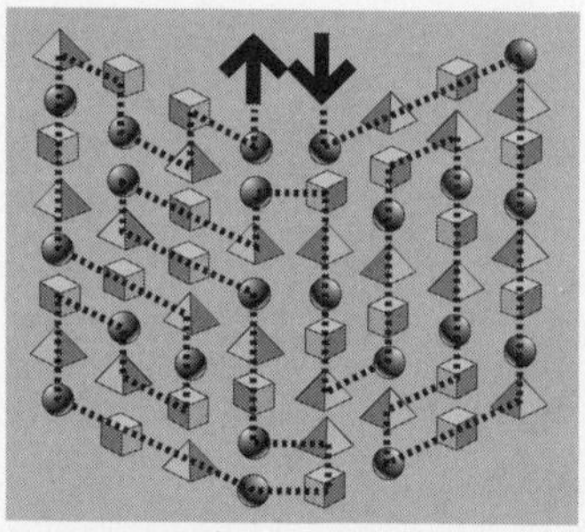

Page 146:

Page 147:

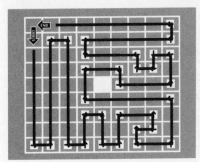

Page 148:

Page 149:

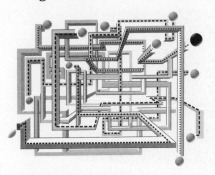

Page 150:

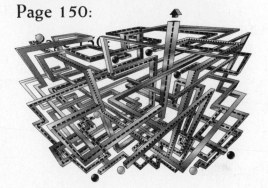

Page 151:

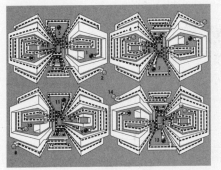

Page 196: 56.

Page 197: Eye brow.

Page 198, a: They are the same size, but the arrows make us think that the lower lizard is bigger than its friend.

Page 198, b: Believe it or not, the little heart is right in the center of the line. If you don't believe it, take a ruler and measure.

Page 199: No, it just looks that way. The vertical and horizontal lines form a perfect square. It's the backgound lines that make it seem as if they are bulging out.

Page 200: No, it too is a perfect square. The background lines are what make the top look narrower.

Page 201: This picture has not been finished, but our brain finishes it for us. We are able to visualize the edges of the pages of this stack of books. This is another example of "closure."

Page 202: Turn the page upside down to see.

Page 203: Turn the page so that the arrow points upward, and you will see one word repeated across the design.

Page 204: These are impossible pencils, so that while you can draw them, you can't use them!

Page 205: Turn the page upside down to find him.

Page 206: It looks like the one on the right, but they are both the same size. What tricks us are the petals around the center.

Page 207: Turn on the light — it's the impossible candelabra! A number of the holders seem to be suspended in mid-air!

Page 208: If you turn the page upside down and look very carefully, you will see the mother's head. The baby's diaper becomes the mother's bandanna.

Page 209: Guess first, then measure. The star is midway between the point and the base.

Page 210, a: They can be seen as either vertical or horizontal.

Page 210, b: The letters flip-flop, so that we can see them pointing up to the right or down to the left.

Page 211, a: Place a small coin on the head of duck #1, and the ducks will seem to move to the right. Now place the coin on the head of duck #2, and the ducks will travel to the left.

Page 211, b: "Minimum."

Page 212: You can make this box open in many different ways—depending on which way you want it to open.

Page 213: The blocks are exactly the same size, though the white one looks bigger. This is another illusion in which the background design confuses us.

Page 214: It's perfect.

Page 215: Turn the page upside down. They're bordering the stem of the glass.

Page 216: They join up perfectly.

Page 217: Our brain is trying to make sense of what we see, so it leaps ahead, closes up the top of the second H, and reads it as an A.

Page 218: The hoop is actually a circle shape, but here it has been drawn as an oval to give the picture the correct perspective.

Page 219: A mouse—or a man's head.

Page 220: No, it's a perfect square. It looks like it's sagging because of the diagonal lines.

Page 221: Either way. This is another design that flip-flops.

Page 222: Slowly bring the page close to your face, and then slowly take the page away from it. There you are—a painless extraction!

Page 223: Just turn the picture upside down.

Page 224: Yes, it's impossible. Count the number of steps. You'll count either 9, 5, or 3.

Page 225: Turn the page upside down to find him.

Page 226: Nothing, it's perfect—but the sides of it look as if they are bending in. That's because of the background of circles.

Page 227: Either one.

Page 228: To find it, just turn the page upside down.

Page 229: The words in the black panels have horizontal symmetry. That means the letters have the same shape on the top and on the bottom.

Page 230: It is a "magic square." Each horizontal line adds up to 264—and so do the vertical and diagonal lines. It also works if you turn it upside down!

Page 231: Yes, but they look different because of the way they have been placed in the angle.

Page 232: Turn the page upside down to see what he looked like.

Page 233: A small gray disk appears in the center of the spokes.

Page 234: Both sets are the same, but lighter objects look bigger than darker ones.

Page 235: Either one.

Page 236: It's an impossible fork! You couldn't make one, but maybe you can draw it…

Page 237: A black cat down a coal mine eating a stick of licorice at midnight.

Page 240. Both mouths are identical. The arrows at the end of the lines confuse us.

Page 241. It reads the same when turned upside down.

Page 242. It says "Have a a Happy Xmas."

Page 243. It depends on how you look at it. Both answers are correct.

Page 244. They are both the same size.

Page 245. It appears to spin.

Page 246. The letter "S."

Page 247. George Washington.

Page 248. They are both the same size. It's the curve that confuses us.

Page 249. Turn the picture upside down. You will see her head wearing a bonnet.

Page 250. Turn the page upside down. Her pet is a pig.

Page 251. It depends on how you look at it. Both answers are correct.

Page 252. They are both the same shade.

Page 253. His head is shown by the "X." See right.

Page 254. The woman places the flower in the man's buttonhole.

Page 255. Yes, the background lines confuse us.

Page 256. The boys are sitting on an impossible staircase. Study the picture. The top stair becomes the middle stair, and vice versa.

Page 257. There are two side profile faces looking at each other. When combined they form a third face that is looking straight ahead.

Page 258. Concentrate on the left-hand side of the picture, starting with her face. You will see a thin lady.

Page 259. It's the letter "G."

Page 260. Although it is the same shade of gray, the part over the white area appears to be darker.

Page 261. Look at the sequence of words. It says "the with." It should be "with the."

Page 263. 1. Shakespeare. 2. He was not for an age but for all time.

Page 264. Turn it upside down. It will then become a "Magic Square" with each row adding up to the number 45.

Page 265. You'll see yourself as others see you. Wink your right eye and see what happens.

Page 266. It all depends on how you look at it.

Page 267. Look at the lion's mane. You will see some of the old British colonies: Canada, India, Australia, New Zealand, and African colonies.

Page 268. Both distances are identical.

Page 269. A white rabbit in a black hat. That's magic!

Page 270. Here are the ten differences: Rabbit's right ear, left eyelash missing, nose filled in, part of right whisker missing, line under right eye missing, right hand is different, two lines under chin missing, line missing from right foot, left thumb is missing, dots under nose missing.

Page 271. Turn the page upside down, and there he is.

Page 272. The print is of two Pierrot clowns. View the page from a distance and watch it change into a gruesome skull.

Page 273. Turn the page upside down. One of the boys is climbing on his beard.

Page 274. It also reads if you look at its reflection in a mirror.

Page 275. Both bulls are identical in size.

Page 276. A dog. Turn the page upside down. The dog can be seen tied up to a tree.

Page 277. You see flashing white stars bouncing among the black stars. Try to focus on these "afterimages" and they will vanish.

Page 278. Both dots are the same size, but lighter objects look bigger than darker ones.

Page 279. The letter "E."

Page 280. The birds go into the cage.

Page 281. It reads the same when turned upside down.

Page 282. No, it doesn't. The sides are parallel all the way to the top. The pattern confuses us.

Page 283. Both lines are the same length. The upright line appears to look longer.

Page 284. Is it an old-fashioned telephone or a picture of two dogs looking at each other? It's both. It all depends on how you look at it.

Page 285. It can be 3, or if you look at the center of the picture you may see an extra one—making a total of 4.

Page 286. 1. The corner numbers are in the wrong corners. 2. The lower number 2 has been reversed. 3. The pip under the reversed number 2 is upside down. 4. The central top and bottom pips should go in opposite directions. 5. There are 3 central pips; there should only be 2.

Page 287. You will see a floating sausage, the size of which depends on how close or how far apart your fingers are. See illustration at the right.

Page 288. Turn the page upside down. Now look at its reflection in a mirror and you will see the correct price is only 20¢.

Page 289. Another macabre picture. Viewed close up, it's a young lady looking at her reflection in a mirror. Viewed from a distance, it's a grinning skull.

Page 290. A monkey. Just turn the page upside down.

Page 291. Flashing gray dots.

Page 292. Yes. To prove it, trace round one of them with a compass.

Page 293. It says "Jack in a a box."

Page 294. There is only one. It's a single continuous line.

Page 295. The numbers 1, 2, 3, 4, 5, 6. Viewing the page from a distance helps.

Page 296. Turn the page upside down. You will see his face formed from the branches.

Page 297. Yes. This is another illusion where the background lines fool us.

Page 298. Either is correct. It all depends on your viewpoint.

Page 299. The arrangement of tree, birds, and boat reminds us of a face.

Page 300. A wise one foresees seasons.

Page 301. Turn the page upside down.

Page 302. The word "COOKBOOK" and those beneath it all read correctly because the letters used to make the words all have horizontal symmetry.

Page 303. Both lines are the same size.

Page 305. You will see a ghostly image of a small silver/gray coin. The size of the coin depends on the size of the rotation.

Page 306. The square gets larger but generally retains the same shape. The lines will get wider.

Page 307. The secret word is "LAUGH." Look at the page at eye level in the direction of the arrow.

Page 308. The ghostly image of a coin appears sandwiched between the two coins you are rubbing.

Page 309. Look at the markings on the cow's back. You will see a map of the United Kingdom.

Page 310. See illustration at the right.

Page 311. It's the word "THE."

Page 312. It disappears. Look at it from all angles. It's gone—just another one of those strange illusions.

Page 313. Turn the page upside down.

Page 314. It looks like an old Asian man. Daniel Webster's shirt forms his forehead.

Page 315. It also works if you turn the image upside down.

Page 316. Hold the page at eye level and slowly bring it towards your face. The snake swallows the bird.

Page 317. It all depends on your viewpoint.

Page 318. General Ulysses Grant.

Page 319. The number 6.

Page 320. Your friend will appear to have one eye in the middle of his or her forehead.

Page 321. You will see an extra rod. Sometimes you may see two extra rods. Amazing!

Page 322. The kaiser. Many of these types were issued during World War I.

Page 323. It appears to follow you, but it's just an illusion.

Page 324. From a distance it looks like a man's head.

Page 325. The one that is on the line, although it looks like the other one.

Page 326. Miss S.I.M. Holland, Albion House, Alcester, Warwickshire.

Page 328. Close up we see a couple of people on a sled. From a distance, it's another of those grinning skulls that were popular in the Victorian era in Europe.

Page 329. You should see 3 balls and 5 glasses. Experiment with different distances.

Page 330. Many people see impressions of very pale colors.

Page 331. Turn the page upside down and it says "Lots o'eggs."

Page 332. It says, "This house is for for sale."

Page 333. Abraham Lincoln.

Page 334. It all depends on your viewpoint. This ambiguous picture "flip-flops."

Page 335. Turn the page upside down. She looks exactly the same.

Page 336. Turn the page upside down to find him.

Page 337. The balloon starts to appear to spin.

Page 338. Both squares are identical. The one with horizontal stripes should appear to be wider. The one with vertical stripes should look taller.

Page 339. You will probably see a small diamond shape in the center of the design surrounded by a bigger diamond shape.

Page 340. You can see this any way you want.

Page 341. Turn the page upside down. The two giants are looking down at the girl.

Page 342. They are parallel. It's the web in the background that confuses us.

Page 343. Turn the number 96 upside down, and it still shows 96.

Page 344. No, it doesn't. The sides are parallel. The design on the frame tricks us.

Page 345. Look at his face. It shows a postman with a sack of mail.

Page 346. Either one is correct. Keep looking at it and it will change.

Page 347. Turn the page so that the arrow points in an upwards direction. The man of the mountain will make his appearance.

Page 348. Look at the reflection of this page in a mirror. The numbers will change into the word "Emperor," which was Napoleon's title.

Page 349. Initially we see 3. But since each head can join onto the different bodies, we get a grand total of 7. Can you work it out?

Page 350. At first glance we assume he's happy, but really he's sad. We are not used to seeing faces upside down. Since the mouth and eyes have been inverted, he seems very weird when we look at him.

Page 351. Either, they are whatever you want them to be.

Page 352. It's both, but most people see the white squares first.

Page 353. Turn the page so that the arrows point upwards. Look above the tiger's eyes and you will see the kaiser looking to the left.

Page 354. Turn the page so that the arrow points downwards. You will see Santa's face. The building in the center forms his nose.

Page 355. The design "flip flops." Take your pick!

Page 356. They are both the same size. Trace one of them and measure it against the other.

Page 357. "X" marks their spot. See illustration at the right.

Page 358. Either is correct. The decision is yours.

Index